SATAN'S
Dirty Little
SECRET

SATAN'S
Dirty Little
SECRET

STEVE FOSS

CREATION HOUSE
A STRANG COMPANY

SATAN'S DIRTY LITTLE SECRET by Steve Foss
Published by Creation House
A Strang Company
600 Rinehart Road
Lake Mary, Florida 32746
www.strangbookgroup.com

Unless otherwise noted, all Scripture quotations are from the New King James Version of the Bible. Copyright © 1979, 1980, 1982 by Thomas Nelson, Inc., publishers. Used by permission.

Scripture quotations marked AMP are from the Amplified Bible. Old Testament copyright © 1965, 1987 by the Zondervan Corporation. The Amplified New Testament copyright © 1954, 1958, 1987 by the Lockman Foundation. Used by permission.

Scripture quotations marked KJV are from the King James Version of the Bible.

Greek word definitions are from *Strong's Exhaustive Concordance of the Bible*, Nashville, TN: Thomas Nelson, 1984.

English word definitions are from *Webster's New World Dictionary*, New York: Simon & Schuster, 1984.

Previously published by Young Warriors International, Keller, TX, ISBN 0-9767917-0-6.

Cover design by Mark Labbe

Library of Congress Control Number: 2007926956
International Standard Book Number: 978-1-59979-204-0

10 11 12 13 14 — 10 9 8 7 6 5
Printed in the United States of America

CONTENTS

FOREWORD

GOD HAS TRULY USED Evangelist Steve Foss to expose some of the most pernicious strategies used by the devil to sideline God's people from fulfilling their potential.

Steve's revelations do not come from an ivory tower, but from face-to-face ministry with tens of thousands of young people and hundreds of thousands on the foreign field and in revival services all over America.

Through Steve's diligence in applying what I taught him—not to deal with the surface, but to go into the spirit world to defeat the enemy—Steve has been rewarded with valuable nuggets of truth to share with the body of Christ on the devil's devices.

—DR. MORRIS CERULLO
PRESIDENT
MORRIS CERULLO WORLD EVANGELISM

INTRODUCTION

THERE ARE TIMES AND seasons when God has opened the eyes of a generation into the spirit realm and revealed hidden truths. We are living in one of those seasons. The Spirit of wisdom and revelation has been opening the eyes of God's people like never before.

The strategies of Satan are being unmasked and the church is about to embark on the greatest season of warfare and victory that it has ever had.

The prophetic nature of this book may make it a bit difficult to digest. The exposing of hidden strongholds is never an easy thing to experience. We all like to feel we are doing pretty well, but God wants us to be free.

The scriptures declare that He who the son sets free is free indeed. (See John 8:36.) Only as we come into truth will we be free.

The truths discussed in this prophetic writing will challenge even the most committed Christian. It is hard hitting at times and fast paced. Take time to read and reread the chapters. Let the Spirit of God bring you into the depths of freedom that only come from deep calling unto deep. (See Psalm 42:7.)

The purpose of this prophetic writing is not to entertain with cute stories and anecdotes. It's to break the back of the enemy's greatest hidden strategy and bring God's people to new levels of freedom.

I pray that the anointing of God be upon you and that the Words of Christ will change you.

CHAPTER 1

THE VISION

For we are not ignorant of his [Satan's] devices.

—2 CORINTHIANS 2:11, KJV

THIS WAS THE DECLARATION of the apostle Paul 2,000 years ago: A declaration of an awareness of the strategies of the enemy—an awareness that has been lost in our day. The traps that the enemy has set for us today are the same as they were 2,000 years ago.

There is nothing new that Satan is doing today. He has not yet had an original idea. He is playing the same game that he played in the Garden of Eden.

Often many of us have thought that if we were in that garden, we surely wouldn't have eaten of the tree of the knowledge of good and evil. (See Genesis 2:17.) Yet every day of our lives we are presented with this same temptation.

Satan challenges us with the same questions. And unfortunately most days we eat of the tree. The fruit binds us, holds us, and dictates to us almost every move.

The war to overcome sin often seems to be an overwhelming task for most. We believe in the finished work of Jesus on the cross, and yet are bound by this continual cycle of yielding to temptation.

Some of you reading this may be feeling a bit smug right now because you think you've got a good handle on sin. You may be in a worse condition. The reality is that the church tends to limit sin to the major moral sins; lying, cheating, adultery, fornication, drunkenness, and such like. Yet the stronghold of sin goes so much deeper in our lives.

Sin affects how we think, what we imagine, what we buy, sell, gather, and give. It affects how we worship, work, and live every aspect of our lives. It leads us into wrong relationships, and to wrongly relate to each other.

Sin dominates our viewpoints, our work ethics, and, most disturbingly, it dominates how we conduct ministry.

The same fruit from that same tree in the garden is being offered to all of us throughout our lives, and we keep eating it, often in the name of God.

The focal point of all of our trouble is the tree of the knowledge of good and evil. This is where it all begins and where it can end. It is what happens here on a daily basis that will determine if the victory that Christ has purchased for us will become a living reality in our lives.

Once again God is about to open the eyes of a generation to the strategies of Satan. By revelation God is going to destroy Satan's most powerful advantage: his ability to operate amidst ignorance.

In this book we are going to uncover Satan's most diabolic strategy—how it works and how it affects our lives. We are going to expose his devices and start down the path of true freedom.

I pray that together we have an Isaiah experience: "Woe is me! for I am undone" (Isa. 6:5). Oh that God would give to us such an encounter with truth that the strongholds of the tree of the knowledge of good and evil are permanently broken in our lives.

The Vision

It was early 1991. I was the youth pastor at Victory Tabernacle in Conyers, Georgia. I had only been on the job for two months when I was invited to speak at the local high school's Christian Bible study. They asked if I would speak two weeks in a row. I readily accepted and began to plan my strategy.

You see this was hard-core Baptist country: Southern Baptist, conservative, don't-give-me-that-Pentecostal-stuff country. I, on the other hand, was a hard-core Holy Ghost tongue-talking, hands-laying, miracle-believing, prophecy-preaching fireball.

I knew that this Bible study had about seventy in attendance every Wednesday morning. I also knew that all except a handful of them came from non-Charismatic/Pentecostal backgrounds.

They gave me about fifteen minutes to speak. My strategy was this. I would preach a basic word on the revelation of Jesus the first week, then hit them with the power of God the second week.

The first week went exactly as I had planned. I preached and they were quite engaged. The revelation anointing flowed strong. By the end of the fifteen minutes they were on the edge of their seats wanting more. I had them right where I wanted them. The next week I was going to blast them.

The day before the second meeting I shut myself off for an extended time of prayer. I knew that if I was going to see a breakthrough in the power of God on this campus, I was going to have to fight some intensive spiritual warfare.

I had been trained by my spiritual father, Dr. Morris Cerullo, in how to tear down strongholds over a region. As I went to prayer I had no idea that what was about to transpire was going to forever change the course of my life.

During that time of prayer I had two visions. The first vision was of the upcoming meeting itself.

I saw a young man whom I had never met. I saw myself calling him to come and stand up front. I then prophesied over him about the call of God on his life. Then I simply spoke the word of the Lord over him and he fell under the power of the Spirit. In the vision I saw his face and exactly where he would be sitting.

When I stood up to speak the next day at the meeting, there he was. And he was sitting exactly where I had seen him in the vision. I preached for a few minutes on experiencing the power of God. Then I called this young man out. He came and stood before me. He was from a non-Spirit-filled background and had no idea what was about to transpire.

I had no helpers with me, so I asked for somebody to come and stand behind him. The volunteer didn't know what was going to happen.

I then proceeded to prophesy over this young man about the call of God on his life to preach. He began to weep. He said that the previous night he told his mother for the first time that he felt God was calling him to be a preacher.

I then looked him in the eyes, standing five feet away from him, and said, "Jesus fill him with your power right now!" As soon as I spoke a wave of God's power swept through that room and hit this young man. He immediately flew backwards under God's power. He landed in the arms of the volunteer who was in total shock.

I turned just in time to see seventy mouths drop open and all heads turn as this young man was being blasted by the power of God. It was all I could do to keep from laughing when I saw the sheer look of shock on their faces.

All together they looked at the young man, then looked at me, and then back at the young man. You could hear gasps all over the room.

I opened the Word to share a couple of scriptures on what just happened. Then the bell rang and they slowly, in shock, filed out of the room. Needless to say I was the talk of the school by the end of the day.

Much transpired at that school over the next several months, but that will have to wait for another book.

As awesome as this was, it was the second vision that changed my life.

After I had this first vision about the young man, I began to go into spiritual warfare prayer. I began to bind specific demon spirits, the ones you would expect to be operating at a high school. I bound lust, drugs, hate, unforgiveness, fornication, pornography, violence, drunkenness, and such like.

I had a fair amount of experience in spiritual warfare and had gained a great sense of what was going on in the spirit realm. I could sense if the stronghold was breaking and when it broke. This day however it felt like I couldn't make any headway. I prayed and prayed, but each of these spirits seemed to not be moved.

As I pressed deeper into prayer I had an open vision. I saw the entire school as if I was standing several hundred yards away. I saw the ground, the campus, the sky, and something very strange.

I saw coming out from under the ground two giant tentacles, one from the left of the campus and the other from the right. They were very thick near the ground and got thinner as they rose higher. The two tentacles interlaced themselves as they met over the top of the center of the campus. They gripped each other powerfully. They were huge.

Then I noticed that attached all along these two tentacles were demon spirits. Each had a name written on them: lust, hate, drunkenness, etc. They each had what looked like two arms with which they grabbed a hold of the tentacles. They didn't hold them on the outside. They were actually rooted into the tentacles themselves.

When I saw them I began to bind them in Jesus' name. I called out lust by name and commanded it to go. I saw this demon of lust get powerfully buffeted and blown backwards. It was like a leaf during a strong gust of wind. It bowed back and shook, but its roots in the tentacles were undamaged. I went from demon to demon and the same thing happened. The more I prayed the harder they got hit.

I started to realize that if they didn't have roots in the two tentacles that my prayers would have easily driven them away from the campus and the students.

As this vision continued I asked the Lord, "What are these two tentacles?" I knew if I could break their power all the others would easily go.

The Lord spoke to me these words that have changed my life. God said, "These are the two demon spirits that all other spirits get their strength from."

These two demon spirits empower all the other demon spirits. This was the mother load of revelation. God then said, "They are the same two spirits that Satan released upon Eve in the garden. They are the same two demon spirits that Satan continues to release today."

I cried out to God, "What are they? What are their names?" I could easily see the names of all the smaller demons, but I couldn't see any names on these. It amazed me how the demons we all think are so big and powerful were actually quite small. Lust, drunkenness, drugs, violence, hatred, and fear were all small and relatively weak without these two giant demon spirits.

I prayed for quite a while. I knew I had to go deep in the spirit to see what was under the surface. After quite a while the vision expanded. Now I could not only see above the ground, but I also saw under the ground below the campus. Each of the tentacles curved back towards each other and nearly touched each other. They looked like giant roots, like a bulb, fat at the bottom and thinner as it got farther away from the root.

Written on these roots were their names.

One was called *Insecurity* and the other was called *Inferiority*.

CHAPTER 2

THE GARDEN

W HEN GOD SHOWED ME the names of these two demon spirits I didn't fully understand. I didn't even really understand what inferiority meant. So I grabbed a dictionary to look up these two words.

The word *insecurity* means "the state of being not secure, not confident, not firm."

The word *inferiority* means "the state of feeling lower in position, stature, or value."

God spoke to me during the vision that these are the same two demon spirits that Satan released upon Eve in the garden. So after looking up the definitions I went to Genesis:

> Now the serpent was more subtle than any beast of the field which the LORD God had made. And he

said unto the woman, Yea, hath God said, Ye shall not eat of every tree of the garden? And the woman said unto the serpent, We may eat of the fruit of the trees of the garden: But of the fruit of the tree which is in the midst of the garden, God hath said, Ye shall not eat of it, neither shall ye touch it, lest ye die. And the serpent said unto the woman, Ye shall not surely die: For God doth know that in the day ye eat thereof, then your eyes shall be opened, and ye shall be as gods, knowing good and evil. And when the woman saw that the tree was good for food, and that it was pleasant to the eyes, and a tree to be desired to make one wise, she took of the fruit thereof, and did eat, and gave also unto her husband with her; and he did eat.

—GENESIS 3:1–6, KJV

Yea, hath God said, Ye shall not eat of every tree of the garden? Thus the set-up begins. The very first step of Satan was to call into question the Word of God. Everything Adam and Eve knew to be true was based solely on what God had spoken to them. God's Word was their only source of truth. They walked with God and talked with God. He gave them the commands concerning the garden and the tree of the knowledge of good and evil.

All of Eve's security was based on the assumption that everything God said was true. God spoke it, and that settled it. She had never even considered questioning the truthfulness of God's Word.

Satan's strategy was to set her up, so he could call into question the truthfulness of God's Word. So he presented a question where he misquoted what God had said. Satan said, "Yea, hath God said, Ye shall not eat of every tree of the garden?" Eve promptly responds with what God had actually said.

"And the woman said unto the serpent, We may eat of the fruit of the trees of the garden: But of the fruit of the tree which is in the midst of the garden, God hath said, Ye shall not eat of it, neither shall ye touch it, lest ye die."

Eve at this point correctly responded to the false statement. But she was now engaged in a conversation in which she shouldn't have engaged. Satan was now ready to release the first of the two demon spirits upon Eve.

"And the serpent said unto the woman, Ye shall not surely die." The first demon spirit was now released. He released upon her *Insecurity*. He knew that her whole security was based upon the absolute trust that everything God said was true. Now all of a sudden she is confronted with the possibility that God was a liar. She began to feel that her whole world was collapsing around her. She felt that she could no longer trust in the sure Word of God. She began to feel *insecure*.

Without hesitation Satan released the second of this dynamic-duo of demon spirits, *Inferiority*. He said, "For God doth know that in the day ye eat thereof, then your eyes shall be opened, and ye shall be as gods, knowing good and evil." Now, not only is she being assaulted by *insecurity*, feeling like everything she knew to be true was called into question, but now Eve believes that she is not who she thought she was.

The Image of God

The Bible declares in Gen. 1:27 "So God created man in his own image, in the image of God created he him; male and female created he them."

Adam and Eve were already in the image of God. They were of full spiritual stature. God never intended for man to have the knowledge of good and evil. Satan took what was good and made it sound bad. Eve now felt that she had been held out on—that she was lacking something. She felt less in position or stature. She now felt *inferior*.

Satan had her right where he wanted her. She felt insecure and inferior. Flooded with these new emotions, she was now overwhelmed and desperate to regain her sense of security and stature.

At this point, although her emotions were overwhelming her, she hadn't actually lost either her real security or stature. She only now believed that she had. With these emotions running high and being assaulted by these two demon spirits, Satan then gave the knockout punch.

He offered to her a solution to her dilemma in the midst of the attack. He said, "**Then your eyes shall be**

opened, and ye shall be as gods, knowing good and evil"
(Gen. 3:5).

"Eve, all you have to do is eat of this fruit and you will
have your security back and you will have your position
back. 'Ye shall be as gods.'"

She reached out and grabbed the fruit. When she bit of
it, in disobedience to God's Word, she lost the very thing
she was trying to regain. She now lost her security and her
stature. She was now fallen.

Satan had succeeded. Man had sinned against God, and
the pure union between God and man was broken. Death
now entered into mankind: spiritual death, emotional
death, relational death, and ultimately physical death.

The partaking of the fruit caused the very thing from
which Eve was trying to get free. From this point on man
would forever fight this same battle. Insecurity and inferiority had now entered into the world, and all the other
demon spirits had their access point upon which to attack
and enslave mankind.

Satan has not changed his strategy. Still to this day
he uses the same two demon spirits to open mankind to
partake of the deadly fruit that enslaves.

Chapter 3

The Sin of Comparison

I NSECURITY AND INFERIORITY ARE the doorways through which every other spirit gets its entrance. In the garden Eve was deceived into believing that God had lied to her and that she wasn't who she thought she was. She felt insecure because she didn't know what the truth was. She felt inferior because she thought that God had misled her and was actually withholding His best.

To this day the same two lies permeate our society. There has been an unending assault on the validity of God's Word. Everywhere you turn the challenge to God's Word is evident.

Simply turn on the evening news or sit-coms and you will hear the questioning of God's Word and principles. People call evil good and good evil. Constantly the values, truths, and authority of the Word of God are challenged and called into question.

Even in churches across America preachers are afraid to preach the unadulterated Word of God. They preach a God of love, but avoid the God of judgment. Isn't it interesting that the serpent also avoided the subject of judgment? He said that God will not judge you. "**Ye shall not surely die**" (Gen 3:4).

We preach a culturally sensitive gospel that often is not God sensitive. We are more interested in attracting people with a positive message than bringing to them the only thing that can make them free.

Eve's only ability to resist the ploys of the enemy was to rely on the truth of God's Word.

Before we go deeper into the revelation of insecurity and inferiority and how it affects almost every part of our lives, we need to look back at the original sin.

Original Sin

Lucifer was the highest of all angels. His beauty was beyond all. There was no one greater than him except God:

> Thou art the anointed cherub that covereth; and I have set thee so: thou wast upon the holy mountain

of God; thou hast walked up and down in the midst
of the stones of fire. Thou wast perfect in thy ways
from the day that thou wast created.

—EZEKIEL 28:14–15, KJV

In this state of absolute perfection a most horrific event took place: Lucifer got his eyes off of God and onto himself:

Thine heart was lifted up because of **thy beauty**, thou hast corrupted thy wisdom by reason of **thy brightness**: I will cast thee to the ground, I will lay thee before kings, that they may behold thee.

—EZEKIEL 28:17, KJV

The scripture declares that iniquity first happened *in* him—in his heart:

Thou wast perfect in thy ways from the day that thou wast created, **till iniquity was found in thee**.

—EZEKIEL 28:15, KJV

Lucifer began to compare himself with God and with others. With God, he saw that God's beauty surpassed his own. With creation, he realized his beauty and brightness was unmatched. He felt inferior to God and superior to others. His solution was simple:

For thou hast said in thine heart, I will ascend into heaven, I will exalt my throne above the stars of God:

> I will sit also upon the mount of the congregation, in
> the sides of the north: I will ascend above the heights
> of the clouds; **I will be like the most High**.
>   —ISAIAH 14:13–14, KJV

He compared himself with another. He wanted to make himself like God. In order for inferiority to exist there must be a comparison.

Suppose a child is born in a remote village and has never had contact with any other people outside of his village. All those in his village have really large ears. Although he sees the large ears, it seems normal to him. But let him get introduced to a village where the people have small ears, and he will immediately begin to compare. He will look at them and notice the difference. Most often he will then either feel inferior or superior to these people.

He has engaged in what I call the sin of comparison. You look to yourself, and then compare with another. This is what Lucifer did in heaven. It is what the serpent had Eve do in the garden:

> For God [elohiym] doth know that in the day ye eat
> thereof, then your eyes shall be opened, and ye **shall
> be as gods** [elohiym], knowing good and evil.
>   —GENESIS 3:5, KJV

It is the same thing that we all do every day of our lives. We are constantly comparing ourselves in all sorts of situations. Stop for a moment and think through the last few hours of your day. How often do we think that this person or that person is smart or dumb, beautiful or homely, nice or mean, rude or kind, arrogant or humble?

We are constantly comparing ourselves to others and others to ourselves. We, as Christians, also do this. We are always measuring ourselves by ourselves. We wish we were more spiritual like so and so, or that we had a bigger church like the one down the street.

We take the other side of the coin on our "successes" and feel we are better than others because of those successes.

The Bible calls comparison a sin. When we measure ourselves by ourselves we are not being wise:

> For we dare not make ourselves of the number, or compare ourselves with some that commend themselves: **but they measuring themselves by themselves, and comparing themselves among themselves, are not wise**.
>
> —2 CORINTHIANS 10:12, KJV

God doesn't want us to compare ourselves with one another. He says this is not wise. In order to enter into comparison we have to be inwardly oriented. We have to be looking to ourselves first. When we head down this path of comparison we end up making a judgment about who we are—about our present state:

> But with me it is a very small thing that I should be judged by you or by a human court. In fact, **I do not**

even judge myself. For I know of nothing against myself, yet I am not justified by this; but He who judges me is the Lord.

—1 CORINTHIANS 4:3–4

Paul realized that he didn't have a true perspective of himself. Even if he thought he was innocent in all areas, he realized that he couldn't have a true understanding outside of God.

When we begin down the path of comparison, we have entered the pathway of deception. We begin to judge by our own perspectives, views, opinions, likes, and dislikes. It leads us to not have our eyes on God, thus we don't see truth.

In every aspect of life we compare things. Something is hot, or something is cold. This is not what I am referring to here. It is when the comparisons cause us to make judgments about ourselves towards others that we have started down this slippery slope.

Comparison is the first step towards insecurity and inferiority. Once insecurity and inferiority take root, they give every other demon spirit a foothold upon which to attach themselves.

The problem always starts when we get our eyes off of God.

CHAPTER 4

THE
ADVERTISING
TRAP

TODAY WE ARE INUNDATED with messages and images at an unprecedented level. Never before in human history has mankind had to deal with such a continual flood tide of information. In just one day of watching television you can be filled with more new information and images than an old-world person may have received in a lifetime.

Everyone is trying to get their message across to us in order to persuade us to their way of thinking. This is no more evident than in the arena of advertising. Advertising has been refined to an art that has the ability to cause the masses to reach out and buy their product, even when the product isn't that good.

In the movie industry the studios have learned how to, with a slick ad campaign, pull in large crowds to the opening weekend of a relatively lame movie.

In the consumer product divisions the advertisers have utilized one of Satan's strategies in order to seduce society into buying their wares. Without trying to demonize consumerism, we must take an honest look at our capitalistic society and the inroads that the enemy has made into it. If we don't begin to recognize Satan's strategies, we will constantly be swayed by them and brought into levels of bondage.

We must first recognize that the American economy is not driven by biblical principles for the purpose of advancing the kingdom of heaven. The American capitalistic system is driven predominately by greed. The recent revelation of major corporations "cooking the books" to falsely pump up their company's value in order that a few may steal millions of dollars is evidence of this greed.

We should not be shocked by this kind of revelation. Much more than this has been going on, but most are never caught. The motivating factor of most companies is to make money at any cost. They are not interested in your personal well being, except where that interest means to them a potential increase in profits.

Once again I must stress than I am not trying to demonize all businesses. There are many godly people in business who operate under a higher calling than simply to make money. If it wasn't for these godly people in our society, things would be much worse. Yet even with these people, much of our western culture is still driven by greed.

In the consumer product industries we find the usage of insecurity and inferiority in advertisement prevalent. They use them to cause you to want to buy their product in order to alleviate your insecurity or inferiority.

For example, in the early 1970's people didn't really have a problem with a person that had an occasional itch on the head. Then a product called Head & Shoulders began to run a very successful campaign showing a handsome man and beautiful woman on a crash course to a romantic meeting. Then suddenly one of them would scratch an itch on their head, and the other would be disgusted and totally put off by this scratching. The message they were sending is: If you have an itch on your head, people will think less of you, (inferiority). Then you would see the same person in the shower using Head & Shoulders. The final scene would be these same two people on another crash course for a romantic meeting. This time, having used Head & Shoulders, there was no more embarrassing itchy, flaky scalp. They met, and it was love at first sight.

Through this advertisement they released a spirit of insecurity and inferiority upon a whole society, and then offered them a fruit to bite into. They basically said, "If you don't buy our product you will miss out on the love of your life. You will be a less attractive person. So here, take this, and eat of it. It will make you wise, strong, powerful, and influential." Sound familiar?

Many companies use this same strategy. Car companies are notorious for this. If you drive such and such car, then you will have the respect of others. Beautiful people will be drawn to you. It will be a status symbol. You are superior with it and inferior without it.

Fashion is driven on this principle. God forbid you get caught with last year's fashion. Why? Is it because the clothes are worn out? Not hardly. It's because the industry has done a masterful job of making us feel insecure and inferior if we don't have the newest, latest, best, etc.

This is how name-brand, fashion-designer clothes can go for so much. "You are better if you wear Tommy Hilfiger. You are more cool if you have Air Jordans." The list goes on and on. Our society is obsessed with how we look. We spend billions of wasted dollars on clothing and apparel that we rarely ever use.

Closets are filled with last year's fashions that won't be used again because we wouldn't be caught dead wearing them: shoes, coats, jackets, hats, etc.

You see the usage of insecurity and inferiority no more prevalent than in the health and fitness industries. We are told through advertising and media that hyper-thin is in.

If you have a little padding on the midsection then you are less attractive. Being less attractive makes you feel insecure and inferior.

Where did we ever get this perverse idea of value? God clearly declared that true beauty is inward. (See 1 Peter 3:3–4.) Yet we ignore His Word and are just as driven as the world into the need to improve our appearance.

We diet to no end. We join health clubs and spend billions in exercise machines, all just to get that perfect body. Who of us wouldn't like to loose a little weight, or trim and tone those flabby areas of our bodies? Or maybe get that six-pack of abs we always see on TV and in magazines. Most of our modern exercise and diet craze isn't really about health, but about personal appearance.

You may say, "Brother Steve, is it wrong to want to look good?"

My response is simple. Look good in whose eyes? Who are you trying to impress? Whose attention are you trying to get? What lack in you are you trying to fill? If insecurity and/or inferiority are at the root of it, then you are once again eating of the tree of the knowledge of good and evil. Once again you are feeding your insecurities and inferiorities.

Now it is not wrong to diet or workout and exercise. These can be very good for you, if they are done for the right reason. The reason must be: to have a healthy body in order to better serve God with. When this is the true motivation you will never be concerned with the size of your biceps, how cut your abs are, or if little areas of cellulose are still there.

Our lives are "hid with Christ in God" (Col. 3:3). We are no longer to live for ourselves, but for Him. Remember, whenever we get our eyes on ourselves and begin to compare, then we have slipped into the trap and are going to be jerked around by the devil once again.

People get plastic surgery, breast implants, and tummy tucks, all to alleviate their insecurities and inferiorities. We are driven by the latest trends. In the 70's it was sexy for a man to have a hairy chest, now it's not. So many men shave their chest in order to have that GQ look.

When I was a young teen, if a guy wore an earring he was gay. Then a gay musician, still in the closet, started to wear an earring in his left ear, stating this made you cool. So multitudes of young men started to wear earrings in the left ear, although the right ear or both was still a sign of being gay. Now guys have earrings in both ears, tongues, lips, belly buttons, chee chees, everywhere. They feel it makes them look more cool. It makes them superior if they have it.

From our hair, clothes, and physical appearance to the products we buy, cars we drive, and on and on, we are a people driven by our need to alleviate our sense of insecurity and inferiority. The advertising community taps into this need and exploits it for their personal gain.

When your eyes are opened and you begin to see this, it can become a little overwhelming. How, when we are surrounded by such an onslaught of temptation to feed our insecurities and inferiorities, do we ever walk free?

In later chapters we will deal in depth with God's solution, but this one verse really sums it up:

> I am crucified with Christ: nevertheless I live; yet not I, but Christ liveth in me: and the life which I now live in the flesh I live by the faith of the Son of God, who loved me, and gave himself for me.
> —GALATIANS 2:20, KJV

The key to total life victory is to stop living for ourselves and live for Him only.

CHAPTER 5

THE MONEY PIT

THE WORKINGS OF INSECURITY and inferiority are also clearly seen throughout the area of finances. For as long as is recorded, man has judged the value of a person based on their wealth. We have, through the centuries, equated wealth with value.

The other day I was watching TV when the movie *Titanic* came on. I was once again horrified when the first-class people were given the limited lifeboat space while the lower class passengers were locked in the decks below.

Our modern day society thinks that we have mostly overcome such blatant discriminations, but the truth is far worse than any want to admit.

Financial security and prosperity is the driving force in much of the western world. Although they are dressed differently the roots are still found in the tree.

On a ministry trip in the early nineties, I was preaching at a friend's church in the downtown area of Detroit. My pastor friend lived in a fairly poor, mostly African-American neighborhood. I went for a walk with him and was shocked to see these little run-down houses all with nice new looking Mercedes and BMW's in the driveway. I couldn't imagine how these people could afford those expensive cars.

I asked my friend, and what he told me opened my eyes. He said that there were two things that were most important to his generation: the car they drove and the clothes they wore. He explained to me that as a kid you would go hungry just so you could have a designer shirt. You would go deep into debt just so you could have that BMW. He told me that his culture had to have these things in order to feel like they were somebody. (Inferiority rears its ugly head!)

Instead of being content with what they had, they would sell themselves into financial slavery to simply have the illusion of prosperity because: Wealth equals value and stature. It makes you superior.

This is not limited at all to any one race. It is the disease of our times; from kids killing other kids so they can have a pair of designer running shoes, to families going into bankruptcy in record numbers just to keep up with the Joneses.

The saying "keeping up with the Joneses" is all about feeding our insecurity and inferiority. My mother has told me stories of when she was a young mother. We lived in a middle class neighborhood and had the perfect *Leave it to Beaver* family. Your house and kitchen floors had to be perfect all the time. She was always so embarrassed that her floors weren't as nice as the neighbors. She'd wax and wax, but they never looked as good. Finally, she found out the secret. The other ladies had a professional service come in. So she had to have the professional service. God forbid that your floors aren't as perfect as the neighbors!

We spend and borrow our way to a sense of security and value. This is why when people are under financial stress, they often pull out the credit cards and buy something. The illusion that is created when we swipe the plastic and don't actually have to pay for it then, gives to us the sense of power and control. It makes us feel that we are wealthier than we are, and thereby momentarily alleviates our sense of insecurity and inferiority.

Often we buy the biggest, most expensive house we can possibly get a loan for. If it weren't for the banks limiting us, many of us would try to get an even more expensive house. We end up with long-term mortgages well into our 70's when we should have owned our homes free and clear in order to pass them on to the next generation.

We are so needy to feel that we are financially succeeding that we will not only mortgage our future, but our children's as well.

We do all of this in direct violation to the Word of God.

We look to wealth and money as a means to feel better about ourselves. Paul gives us another way to live:

> Not that I speak in regard to need, for I have learned in whatever state I am, to be content.
> —PHILIPPIANS 4:11

We go into debt to feed our desires or our families' lusts but scriptures say:

> Owe no man anything, but to love one another.
> —ROMANS 13:8

I am not saying that God doesn't want us to have nice things, but why do we want them? Is it to feed some deep sense of insecurity and inferiority? So often it is. God says for us to be content, but many of us want so much more— the newest car, latest gadget, today's fashion, finest house, and on and on. Instead of "Seek ye first the kingdom of God, and his righteousness; and all these things shall be added unto you" (Matt. 6:33, KJV).

The care for things can be one of the greatest enemies of the Word in your life:

> Now he who received seed among the thorns is he
> who hears the word, and the **cares of this world** and
> the **deceitfulness of riches choke the word**, and **he
> becomes unfruitful**.
>
> —MATTHEW 13:22

Why does he become unfruitful? Because of two things:

1. "The cares of this world," meaning the distractions of this present age.

2. "The deceitfulness of riches," meaning the delusion that wealth and possessions provide worth and safety.

These two things will choke out the Word of God—make it fruitless in our lives.

This battle is one of our most challenging, because we have believed a lie that wealth and possessions bring a sense of value and security. We keep eating from the tree the fruit of wealth, or the illusion of wealth, to give our lives value. We have bowed down to the god of mammon.

One of the great dangers of this is that those who are in the church can use the promises of God to serve their lust for things. They actually try to make God their servant in order to get what they really feel they need—wealth.

God warns us of this:

> No one can serve two masters; for either he will hate
> the one and love the other, or else he will be loyal to
> the one and despise the other. You cannot serve God
> and mammon.
>
> —Matthew 6:24–25

In life you will serve either God or mammon. The other will be your servant. Many who think they are serving God are actually serving mammon. They look to mammon as their source.

How many times have we said, "All I need is some more money and I can do this or that?" So often we have looked to money and wealth as the "answer" to our problems. We think that more money will solve many of our problems.

We then start hearing teaching about biblical prosperity (which, by the way, I truly do believe and teach strongly). However, just like preaching deliverance to an alcoholic while giving him a drink is futile, so is preaching prosperity to those who serve mammon. Those who look to money to give them a sense of value and security will misuse the truth of biblical prosperity to feed their insecurities and inferiorities.

You can hardly turn on the TV without seeing an infomercial advertising some new business opportunity that will give you two things: security and the good life—in other words, value. We buy their programs, join their clubs, and attend their meetings all in the hope of getting some financial security and freedom.

We as Christians talk ourselves into how we will be able to help so many other people once we get the money from this program or business. Somewhere deep in the root of most of this is a devastating lie: money is the answer.

God can provide all you and I need without money. He may, and often does, use the tool of money, but He and He alone is the answer. He is our source.

That is what Jesus was dealing with in Matthew chapter 6. You cannot love God and mammon:

> **No one can serve two masters**; for either he will hate the one and love the other, or else he will be loyal to the one and despise the other. You cannot serve God and mammon. **Therefore I say to you, do not worry about your life**, what you will eat or what you will drink; nor about your body, what you will put on. Is not life more than food and the body more than clothing? Look at the birds of the air, for they neither sow nor reap nor gather into barns; yet your heavenly Father feeds them. Are you not of more value than they? Which of you by worrying can add one cubit to his stature? So why do you worry about clothing? Consider the lilies of the field, how they grow: they neither toil nor spin; and yet I say to you that even Solomon in all his glory was not arrayed like one of these. Now if God so clothes the grass of the field, which today is, and tomorrow is thrown into the oven, will He not much more clothe you, O you of little faith? Therefore do not worry, saying, 'What shall we eat?' or 'What shall we drink?'

or 'What shall we wear?' **For after all these things the Gentiles seek**. For your heavenly Father knows that you need all these things. **But seek first the kingdom of God and His righteousness, and all these things shall be added to you**. Therefore do not worry about tomorrow.

—MATTHEW 6:24–31

If we are looking to money as our answer, we have fallen into the trap of the tree. We have believed the lie that God is not sufficient, that He alone cannot sustain us:

I know how to be abased, and I know how to abound. Everywhere and in all things I have learned both to be full and to be hungry, both to abound and to suffer need. **And my God shall supply all your need** according to His riches in glory by Christ Jesus.

—PHILIPPIANS 4:12–13

Paul had come to the true understanding that God was his source, not wealth. So if he had it, he was content. If he didn't he was content, for he knew God would supply all his needs.

God is our source; money is our servant. The battle of the deception of false security and value from wealth is why Jesus said:

It is easier for a camel to go through the eye of a needle than for a rich man to enter the kingdom of God.

—MATTHEW 19:24

Jesus never had a problem with somebody having wealth. He simply understood how easy it was to feed any insecurity and inferiority with wealth. Jesus knew the trap and that for many the deception of false security and value from wealth would keep them from being able to look to God as their source.

This is why the rich young ruler went away sad. His trust was in wealth, not God. Jesus gave him an opportunity to be delivered, but instead he walked away from Christ and embraced his riches. (See Matthew 19:22.)

It wasn't that Jesus glorifies being poor, for He often spoke of the promise of abundance and blessings for those who would fully obey God. He was dealing with the tree of the knowledge of good and evil in this rich man's life.

I believe one of the reasons that God at times speaks to us to give a sacrificial offering, is to keep Him as the source and not our checking account.

Ask God to search your heart. Ask Him to expose the secret trust you have in money and wealth. Break the stronghold of the tree over your life that exists through wealth and money.

CHAPTER 6

IDENTITY

IN EVERY ASPECT OF life the workings of insecurity and inferiority are apparent. It is the root of most divisions within the body of Christ.

You see it when believers are separated one from another over doctrine. Now I do believe that doctrine is important, and there are some doctrines that, if they are not in proper order, can lead to much confusion and damage within the body. However, there are very few that should ever produce isolation and separation from one another. Only those which are truly doctrines of demons, which deny the deity of Christ and the completeness of His blood sacrifice to provide salvation for all who make Him Lord, should ever cause us to separate. Most all of the rest, which most splits are based on, should never produce isolation and separation.

The reason they do is because of insecurity and inferiority. Most people don't own their doctrines, but are owned by them. What I mean is this: they actually gain their sense of identity from the doctrines themselves. It becomes who they are.

For example one might say, "I am a Calvinist." Another might say, "I am a Pentecostal." While another might say, "I am a Fundamentalist." These titles in and of themselves aren't bad, if all they were stating was a description of our form of Christian practice; however, they have become much more than that. They become our identity.

We gain a sense of security and belonging with those who are like-minded. We gain a sense of value from our belief system and doctrine. We actually begin to feel a bit better about ourselves, because we have been enlightened more than someone else. It gives us a sense of power and superiority. It could escalate to a haughty spirit, but more often it is much more subtle than that.

It is just a feeling of being better because you're right. We all like being right. We all like being ahead of the rest, even just a little bit. We like having the sense of power and control from having an insight into truth. It increases our personal sense of worth and we begin to gain our identity from it.

Once we've crossed the deadly bridge of gaining our identity from doctrine, the trap of the tree has once again snared us.

Whatever you gain your identity from you will defend, protect, and promote!

Once you gain your identity from something it then owns you. If you gain your identity from doctrine, then it owns you. You *will* defend it, protect it, and promote it. Because in so doing you are defending, protecting, and promoting yourself, your value, and your sense of worth.

We have all seen this at work in our churches. Somebody believes that they have come into a new revelation. They heard somebody preach or read a book. The doctrine touched them on some deep emotional level and they have now embraced it. They have gained a new feeling of value. They begin to promote this doctrine to others and are surprised that everybody doesn't see it the way they do. Some of their brothers and sisters challenge this new doctrine. The person becomes defensive and upset. They then begin to fight to protect and defend the doctrine. This leads to strife. Often the person with the new doctrine begins to line up with the accuser of the brethren and starts to attack his brothers and sisters by calling them religious or deceived.

This attack comes as a defensive mechanism. It's not to truly bring about truth, but to protect their new-found identity. It is all about self-preservation. Often they will work to gather a small group who also believe this new way. They meet together informally and talk about how the pastor needs to be delivered or needs a new revelation.

Even if they are correct, they enter into covenant with a seditious spirit.

Instead of embracing humility because of their new revelation, they begin to lay the groundwork for a coup. If they can't manipulate the existing church to go their way, they will feel "led by the Lord" to leave. A church split has now become fully grown. They have isolated themselves from others in the body.

The spirit of pride has been working mightily, as they pat themselves on the back for becoming free from that formerly oppressive, religious church. They now "have the truth" and will build God's kingdom "the way God wanted" it to be done.

Satan is now rejoicing. Once again the spirits of insecurity and inferiority have done their job and led people to eat from the tree of the knowledge of good and evil. Once again man has become bound and the fruit of the enemy is spreading.

Even if the doctrine that these people have is correct, they allowed it to own them. They got their identity from it and fell into Satan's trap.

God may have been trying to restore a truth, but instead evil polluted it.

Recently I was at a youth camp when a teenage girl asked me if there was anything wrong with getting a tattoo. I knew she really didn't want an answer, just a justification for an action she had already determined in her heart to do.

I still decided to respond to her by leading her to some principles. I said, "In the Old Testament..."

As soon as I said that she cut me off and said, "That's the Law. We're not under the Law."

I responded, "That is your wrong and ignorant thinking talking. Jesus didn't come to do away with the Law. He came to fulfill it. Murder is still sin. What you don't understand is that in all the Law are principles; spiritual laws that are still in effect today."

I continued, "Even the sanitary laws like going so many paces outside your tent to dig a hole to go to the bathroom in still have underlying principles that if violated today will bring a form of judgment. The sanitary laws were given because man had no understanding of germs and microorganisms. If you go to the bathroom even now and don't wash your hands, or allow the toilet to overflow and not be cleaned, germs and disease will spread. The specific regulation may no longer be required, but the underlying truth that God was getting at still does. The same goes for the principle found in the Word about taking on the markings of the heathen nations."

> You shall not make any cuttings in your flesh for the
> dead, nor tattoo any marks on you: I am the LORD.
> —LEVITICUS 19:28

I continued to explain that the principle was that we were not to take on the identifying marks of those groups that were enemies of God. I said to her, "What would you think of me if I showed up to preach wearing a satanic pentagram and some upside down crosses? Would you have a problem with me?"

She said, "Yes."

I immediately responded, "How dare you judge me! You don't know my heart." In response to the shocked look on her face, I concluded by saying, "Of course you know my heart by what I wear. Even if I don't practice the practices of those who wear these things, I have made a choice to publicly identify with them. There is no difference between that and wearing a swastika. The principle is to not take on the identifying markings of those who don't serve God."

This is why there is no such thing as a Christian gangster or Christian gothic. These groups, by their core beliefs, oppose the message of the Gospel. They are rooted in rebellion and death. You can apply this to many counter culture groups out there.

Slapping the name of Jesus on rebellion doesn't make it good. It doesn't make it holy:

> I have stretched out My hands all day long to a rebellious people, Who walk in a way that is not good, **According to their own thoughts**; A people who provoke Me to anger continually to My face; Who sacrifice in gardens, And burn incense on altars of brick; Who sit among the graves, And spend the night in the tombs; Who eat swine's flesh, And the

broth of abominable things is in their vessels; **Who say, 'Keep to yourself, Do not come near me, For I am holier than you!'** These are smoke in My nostrils, A fire that burns all the day. Behold, it is written before Me: I will not keep silence, but will repay—Even repay into their bosom.

—ISAIAH 65:2–6

Let's look at these verses one by one, for there is great revelation here. First God said that these people—His people—walk in a way that is not good, according to their own thoughts. They thought they were pleasing God, though. They did these things to His face. These weren't a people who blatantly rebelled against God. They were deceived to believe that their practices were good. They not only thought that their practices were good, but that they were more holy than others who didn't practice the way they did:

Who say, 'Keep to yourself, Do not come near me, For I am holier than you!'

—ISAIAH 65:5

What were they doing that so displeased God that He said, "These are smoke in My nostrils, A fire that burns all the day." and "I will not keep silence, but will repay."

Verses 3–4 give us the answer:

A people who provoke Me to anger continually to My face; Who sacrifice in gardens, And burn incense on altars of brick; Who sit among the graves, And spend the night in the tombs; Who eat swine's flesh, And the broth of abominable things is in their vessels.

If you study this you will see that what they did was to imitate the heathen practices for worship and tried to do it that way towards God. They looked to the culture of the day and changed their worship practices to match the culture that surrounded them.

Throughout Jewish history we see this time and time again: God's people trying to fit in with the culture of the day and using their practices to try and worship God. Often they wanted to be like the others. They just wanted to fit in.

In Moses' day they wanted a graven image. In Samuel's day they wanted a king like the other nations. (See Exodus 32, 1 Samuel 8.) Over and over God's people were tempted by insecurity and inferiority. They wanted to be like others, but not completely abandon God. So they incorporated the world's practices into the worship of God.

In church history this has also happened with equally devastating results. The Catholic Church, in an attempt to relate to the heathens, incorporated statues and prayers to the dead (the saints). These were heathen practices that the church slapped Jesus' name on in an attempt to relate and identify.

All of this flies in the face of God and His Word. He is a jealous God and He wants to be the sole focus of our affections:

> You shall have no other gods before Me. You shall not make for yourself a carved image—any likeness of anything that is in heaven above, or that is in the earth beneath, or that is in the water under the earth; you shall not bow down to them nor serve them. **For I, the Lord your God, am a jealous God**.
>
> —EXODUS 20:3–5

> You shall love the LORD your God with all your heart, with all your soul, and with all your strength.
>
> —DEUTERONOMY 6:5

God wants us to get our identity from Him and Him alone:

> And these words which I command you today shall be in your heart. You shall bind them as a sign on your hand, and they shall be as frontlets between your eyes.
>
> —DEUTERONOMY 6:6, 8

He wanted His people to publicly, visibly, and clearly be identified with Him and His Word.

Whatever you get your identity from you will defend, protect, and promote. Too often God's people are getting their identity from anything and everything other than Christ. This will only further lead them down the path of bondage to insecurity and inferiority.

CHAPTER 7

CAUGHT IN THE MIDDLE

I NSECURITY AND INFERIORITY HAVE torn many great men of God from their positions of honor and anointing. They started so strong and humble before God, but ended their lives in destruction.

We have seen this throughout the history of man. So many anointed and appointed servants of God end up eating from the tree, to their own demise.

Probably one of the best examples in Scripture is in the story of Saul and David:

> Now the LORD had told Samuel in his ear the day before Saul came, saying, "Tomorrow about this time I will send you a man from the land of Benjamin, and

> you shall **anoint him commander over My people Israel**, that **he may save My people** from the hand of the Philistines; for I have looked upon My people, because their cry has come to Me."
>
> —1 SAMUEL 9:15–16

> Then Samuel took a flask of oil and poured it on his head, and kissed him and said: "Is it not because **the Lord has anointed you commander over His inheritance?**"
>
> —1 SAMUEL 10:1

Saul was anointed king over Israel and the Spirit of God came upon him. But Saul was ruled by insecurity and inferiority. He was insecure about his position with the hearts of the people, so he began to eat of the fruit of the fear of man. It caused him to disobey God:

> Samuel also said to Saul, "The LORD sent me to anoint you king over His people, over Israel. Now therefore, heed the voice of the words of the LORD. Thus says the LORD of hosts: 'I will punish Amalek for what he did to Israel, how he ambushed him on the way when he came up from Egypt. **Now go and attack Amalek, and utterly destroy all that they have, and do not spare them. But kill both man and woman, infant and nursing child, ox and sheep, camel and donkey.'**"
>
> —1 SAMUEL 15:1–3

Saul did not obey the command of God:

> And Saul attacked the Amalekites, from Havilah all the way to Shur, which is east of Egypt. He also took Agag king of the Amalekites alive, and utterly destroyed all the people with the edge of the sword. **But Saul and the people spared Agag and the best of the sheep, the oxen, the fatlings, the lambs, and all that was good, and were unwilling to utterly destroy them**. But everything despised and worthless, that they utterly destroyed.
>
> —1 SAMUEL 15:7–9

Saul reports to Samuel that he has obeyed the Lord:

> But Samuel said, **"What then is this bleating of the sheep in my ears, and the lowing of the oxen which I hear?"** And Saul said, **"They have brought** them from the Amalekites; for **the people spared the best of the sheep and the oxen**, to sacrifice to the LORD your God; and **the rest we have utterly destroyed."**
>
> —1 SAMUEL 15:14–15

Now Saul begins to make excuses and justify his disobedience. Sounds like the same thing Adam did in the garden:

> Then the man said, **"The woman whom You gave to be with me, she gave me of the tree, and I ate."**
>
> —GENESIS 3:12

Like Adam blamed Eve, Saul started to blame the people. He tries to minimize his disobedience by pointing to the parts where he did obey God. For those of us who have children, how often have we heard from this particular fruit of the tree? "But I mostly obeyed," they'll say.

Samuel continues to press Saul to expose the reality of his sin. Saul still is quite insistent that he is innocent:

> And Saul said to Samuel, "**But I have obeyed the voice of the Lord**, and gone on the mission on which the LORD sent me, and brought back Agag king of Amalek; I have utterly destroyed the Amalekites.
>
> —1 SAMUEL 15:20

Saul also continued to blame the people:

> **But the people took of the plunder**, sheep and oxen, the best of the things which should have been utterly destroyed, to sacrifice to the LORD your God in Gilgal."
>
> —1 SAMUEL 15:21

After pressing Saul a third time and delivering to him the Word of the Lord, Saul finally admits his guilt and the reason:

> Then Saul said to Samuel, "I have sinned, for I have transgressed the commandment of the LORD and your words, **because I feared the people and obeyed their voice**.
>
> —1 SAMUEL 15:24

This was the beginning of the end for King Saul. He was so insecure about his relationship with the people that instead of commanding the people to destroy *all* the people and spoils, he cowered to their desires and ended up disobeying God. This has happened time and again throughout history.

Saul had given Satan a foothold by listening to his lies and not trusting that God had placed him as king and God could keep him there. Instead Saul reached for the fruit of the fear of man, then disobedience. He fell trap to political pressure and ended up losing his standing with God.

The root was now well established in Saul. The Spirit of God had departed from Saul who desperately wanted to keep his kingdom. Into this scene now comes God's newly anointed servant David.

The hand and favor of God was mightily upon David. He won the battle against Goliath, and was now becoming a great warrior in Saul's army. You would think this would make Saul happy and rejoice. But the person controlled by insecurity and inferiority will grab for some fruit from the tree:

> And it came to pass as they came, when David was returned from the slaughter of the Philistine, that the women came out of all cities of Israel, singing and dancing, to meet king Saul, with tabrets, with joy, and with instruments of music.
>
> —1 Samuel 18:6, kjv

> And the women answered one another as they played, and said, **Saul hath slain his thousands, and David his ten thousands**. [Comparison comes

in and opens the door for insecurity and inferiority] **And Saul was very wroth, and the saying displeased him**; and he said, They have ascribed unto David ten thousands, and to me they have ascribed but thousands [**In other words they say "I am inferior to David"**]: and what can he have more but the kingdom? [**I feel insecure. David may steal the kingdom from me. I view him as a threat to my security and value or stature.**] And Saul eyed David **from that day and forward**. And … there was a javelin in Saul's hand. And Saul cast the javelin; for he said, I will smite David even to the wall with it. And David avoided out of his presence twice. And **Saul was afraid of David**, [**insecurity**] because **the Lord was with him**, [**inferiority**] and was departed from Saul. Therefore Saul removed him from him.

—1 SAMUEL 18:7–13, KJV

You can go throughout the ministry today and find example after example of this very thing happening. Ministers have become afraid of other ministers stealing their ministry from them. They are believing a lie. It affects how they operate. It affects whom they surround themselves with and how they treat others.

There are also many young ministries that are filled with insecurity and inferiority. They feel like older ministers aren't giving them the opportunities that they should. They feel that these older leaders aren't opening the doors for them, so they start to grab the fruit of a critical spirit. On and on it goes. God's leaders keep believing lies from the serpent that make them feel insecure and/or inferior. With fruit in hand the enemy skillfully presents it to the leaders, and once again they partake of it.

At times and seasons we come to the realization that what we are doing is wrong. We seemingly repent, but have never truly gone to the root cause. We are only recognizing the fruit. As a result, the problem will come back. This is also what happened to Saul:

> And Jonathan spake good of David unto Saul his father, and said unto him, Let not the king sin against his servant, against David; **because he hath not sinned against thee, and because his works have been to thee-ward very good**: For he did put his life in his hand, and slew the Philistine, and the LORD wrought a great salvation for all Israel: thou sawest it, and didst rejoice: wherefore then wilt thou sin against innocent blood, to slay David without a cause? **Saul hearkened unto the voice of Jonathan: and Saul sware, As the Lord liveth, he shall not be slain**. And Jonathan called David, and Jonathan showed him all those things. **And Jonathan brought David to Saul, and he was in his presence, as in times past**.
>
> —1 SAMUEL 19:4–7, KJV

Saul recognized he was wrong and changed his ways—*for a season*:

> And there was war again: and David went out, and fought with the Philistines, and slew them with a

> great slaughter; and they fled from him. And **Saul sought to smite David even to the wall with the javelin**; but he slipped away out of Saul's presence, and he smote the javelin into the wall: and David fled, and escaped that night. Saul also sent messengers unto David's house, to watch him, and to slay him in the morning: and Michal David's wife told him, saying, If thou save not thy life tonight, tomorrow thou shalt be slain.
>
> —1 SAMUEL 19:8, 10–11, KJV

Saul had made the pledge to not harm David. Then David began to walk in his anointing again:

> …and David went out, and fought with the Philistines, and slew them with a great slaughter; and they fled from him…

Saul, filled again with rage, tried to kill David. The reason he did this is that Saul never dealt with the roots of insecurity and inferiority, even though on several occasions he admitted that what he was doing was wrong and he seemingly repented.

Saul's life reflects so many today. They start out under the anointing, but end up believing a lie. They fall prey because in their hearts there was an open door of insecurity and inferiority.

We must go deep in the spirit to the root cause if we are going to be free.

CHAPTER 8

THE TRAPPED CHRISTIANS

A S GOD HAS CONTINUED to unveil this amazing truth into my life, I see the working of insecurity and inferiority in almost every facet of life. I see in my own life the many arenas that it plays such a major role, and yet often does it in a stealth way. Because these two demon spirits are the footholds of many other spirits, often we only see the most visible ones and not the roots.

In the vision that God had given to me, I could see the two tentacles to which all the other spirits were attached, but I was unable to identify them until I went much deeper in the spirit. I clearly saw the names of the demons of fear, hate, lust, rage, drugs, etc. However, it wasn't until

I pressed in much deeper in the Spirit that my eyes were opened, and I saw under the surface to the real roots that gave all these other spirits strength.

I have found that this vision was so accurate in not only revealing to me what the root was, but also how hidden and hard to identify it so often is. Many Christians struggle and fight with so many strongholds. They go to church, read books, get prayed for, even attend deliverance services; but so often they continue to struggle with fear, anger, rage, lust, pornography, homosexuality, unforgiveness, greed, intimidation, and many others.

We often see people come into the church with these struggles and never truly get free. They come for a while, and then usually end up in one of three camps.

The first camp is the camp of condemnation. They go to a church that preaches righteous and holy living. They know it to be the truth, but can never seem to get it to work out in their own lives. Try as they may, they live their lives in a state of continual condemnation, always feeling unworthy and unable to obtain. But because of their love for God and/or their fear of hell, they continue in the church, often putting on the mask of religion so that nobody sees the struggles they are going through.

The second group also continues in a church, but they find a church that preaches a gospel of "grace". It's not true grace, but a license to sin. They hear messages on how to have a good career and how to keep a positive attitude. The church avoids pointing out the spiritual strongholds, and often justifies them by a doctrine that says, "As long as we're in the flesh, we can't be free from sin." Although this brings a freedom from the sense of condemnation, it doesn't bring the freedom that Christ died for us to experience.

The third group of people is the largest. They simply give up. They stop trying to fight and eventually leave the church all together. Many feel that the church is an outdated, irrelevant institution that doesn't have any real answers for them. Unfortunately, in some ways they're right. Oh the gospel has all the answers and is truly relevant, but what many churches present today isn't the full gospel.

I attended a major, black, charismatic church in the Chicago area. The music was high-powered and the atmosphere electrified. Every month they would have a deliverance service. Now I believe in the delivering power of God, and God has used me to cast demons out of hundreds of people. I have seen, in a single service, over 200 people manifest demons, and at the name of Jesus all 200 get instantly delivered.

However, in this service the regular church people who have been prayed for over and over again all came for another "deliverance." They showed up with their little brown paper bags, so they could throw up the demons. You would hear the people start to choke and cough, some even gag. They would go through this ritual month after month, but never seem to get truly free.

The Word is clear. "Therefore if the Son makes you free, you shall be free indeed" (John 8:36).

I'm not saying these people aren't wrestling with demonic powers, but where is the freedom? Is it possible that, just like in my vision, they keep going after the surface spirits and fail to deal with the real root that gives that stronghold its strength?

I want to address an issue here. I have been speaking of these demon spirits and demonic powers having access because of insecurity and inferiority. I am not predominantly talking about demon possession. I am speaking of the kind of demonic influence that all of us face all of the time. Although demon possession is real and needs to be dealt with, most of what we deal with falls under the category of the works of the flesh.

These are those things that are the result of the fall of man and the working of sin. They are, however, fueled by the demon powers at work in the world. As Paul says:

> **For we wrestle not against flesh and blood, but against principalities, against powers, against the rulers of the darkness of this world, against spiritual wickedness in high places.**
>
> —Ephesians 6:12, kjv

Our fight is both internal and external. It's this one, two punch that confuses and holds captive so many believers.

The enemy knows that unless he can gain a stronghold in the thinking of a man, he cannot truly control that man. The enemy has no strength over us as believers, except that which we give him through submitting and agreeing with his lies. The battlefield is two fold and must be fought on both fronts. It is in the heavenlies and it is in our minds.

CHAPTER 9

LOCATE OUR ENEMY

T{RUE FREEDOM IN CHRIST} will only come when we have a revelation on two key areas of spiritual warfare:

1. Locate our enemy.
2. Locate the battlefield.

These two are keys to successful warfare. In recent years the United States has been in a war on terror. This is a most difficult war, because the two primary elements of successful warfare are so hard to clearly identify. First we are having a hard time locating our enemy. As of the writing of this chapter, we have yet to locate Osama Bin

Laden. He is still at large somewhere in the world giving some guidance to those who want to destroy America and Israel.

We also have a second problem. We don't know where in the world the next battle is going to be fought. Will they attack New York again with planes, an embassy in Africa with car bombs, or a suicide bomber in a crowded market place? There are so many ways that they can attack with little or no warning.

The problem with the war on terror is that we are having a difficult time locating our enemy and locating the battlefield.

We have the overwhelming power to destroy our enemy, but if we can't locate these two key areas we will never be free.

This is why we are spending so much time and resources on *intelligence*.

Intelligence is the key to winning the war. If we get the right intelligence, we can win. If not we are still vulnerable.

All truth is parallel.

The same is true in spiritual warfare. The key is spiritual intelligence. If we can locate our enemy and the battlefield, we have the overwhelming firepower to easily defeat our enemy.

Satan is terrified of you discovering these two keys to warfare. That is exactly what you are discovering now. By revelation we have discovered one of Satan's best-kept secrets: *insecurity* and *inferiority*. We have located our deeply hidden enemy. Now that we have located our enemy, we are halfway to victory.

The second key is to locate the battlefield. This is revealed to us in 2 Corinthians:

> (For the weapons of our warfare [are] not carnal, but mighty through God to **the pulling down of strong holds**;) **Casting down imaginations**, and every high thing that exalteth itself against the knowledge of God, **and bringing into captivity every thought** to the obedience of Christ.
>
> —2 CORINTHIANS 10:4–5, KJV

The battlefield is in our minds. Despite all of the work of the enemy in the atmosphere, if he has no access to our minds, we will have total victory. If we can win in the battle of the mind, we can win the battle of life.

Satan sets up strongholds in our thought life. It is the *same* strategy that he used on Eve in the garden. He didn't have the power to take her captive. He had to convince her to willingly surrender herself to his control and influence. He had to cause her to want to follow him. He had to plant seeds into her mind that she would act on—thoughts that were lies.

She had to become *deceived.*

If he could only convince her of his lie, then he could lead her into a path of destruction and bondage through disobedience. He needed to establish a *stronghold* in her mind:

> Now the serpent was more subtle than any beast of the field which the LORD God had made. And he said unto the woman, Yea, hath God said, Ye shall not eat of every tree of the garden? And the woman said unto the serpent, We may eat of the fruit of the trees of the garden: But of the fruit of the tree which is in the midst of the garden, God hath said, Ye shall not eat of it, neither shall ye touch it, lest ye die. And the serpent said unto the woman, **Ye shall not surely die** [**stronghold of Insecurity**]: For God doth know that in the day ye eat thereof, then your eyes shall be opened, and **ye shall be as gods** [**stronghold of Inferiority**], knowing good and evil. **And when the woman saw that the tree was good for food, and that it was pleasant to the eyes, and a tree to be desired to make one wise** [**Eve was now deceived. She believed the lie that the tree was good and pleasant and desirable**.], she took of the fruit thereof, and did eat, and gave also unto her husband with her; and he did eat.
>
> —GENESIS 3:1–6, KJV, EMPHASIS ADDED

These three results of deception led Eve down the path of destruction:

1. She *felt* that the fruit was *good*.
2. She *felt* that the fruit would be *pleasant*.

3.   She *felt* that the fruit was something to be *desired*.

All three of these *feelings* were lies. The tree was never good for man. It has led to thousands of years of death, destruction, and chaos. But these three things reveal to us an amazing truth about human nature:

We are drawn towards pleasure and flee from pain.

God made us that way. Even in the garden He warned them of the *pain* of disobedience:

> And the woman said unto the serpent, We may eat of the fruit of the trees of the garden: But of the fruit of the tree which is in the midst of the garden, **God hath said, Ye shall not eat of it, neither shall ye touch it, lest ye die**.

Satan's strategy was to get her to believe a lie; because once she believed the lie, her emotions would begin to lead her down a wrong path.

For years preachers have said that we are not to live by feelings. This is a fallacy. Man is always driven by his emotions and always will be. Emotions are your primary force of motivation and energy. Scientists say that 70 percent of your physical energy comes from your emotions.

We are *not* to deny our emotions. We are to make sure they are motivating us toward godly things and not the works of the flesh.

Emotions are all based in thoughts. Your thoughts determine what you feel. If what you think is correct, then what you feel will be correct. If your thinking is wrong, then your feelings *will* be wrong.

Eve started to think through the eyes of insecurity and inferiority. She believed that God had lied to her and was withholding something good from her. She felt pain. She wanted to feel pleasure again. She felt that if she ate of the fruit she would be free from the pain and have pleasure once again. She was deceived.

What she felt was a lie based upon her wrong thinking.

We have so much to learn from Eve! This strategy of Satan continues today. Through the feelings of pain from insecurity and inferiority, and the intense desire to alleviate that pain and acquire the pleasure of security and worth, Satan has set us up to follow him to do almost anything.

If the feelings of pain for not doing something and the desire for pleasure to do it are strong enough, we will do just about anything.

We see this even in the horrible tragedy of suicide. Somewhere in the person's mind they have become convinced that the pain of living is greater than the potential pain of killing themselves, and that the pleasure of being free from the pressures of this life is stronger than the pleasure to live. They then become willing to kill themselves. Their deception has gone so deep that this form of escapism is taken. In a much less dramatic degree people do this all the time. We escape into drugs, alcohol, sex, pornography, riotous living, and such like.

People are draw towards these things because they become convinced that these things, even though morally wrong, are actually *good* for them. They believe that these things will provide *pleasure* and are to be *desired*.

Even Christians fall into this trap all of the time. Sometimes it's as small as overeating. They know that that extra donut won't do them any good. They know that overeating can bring serious health risks and even early death. But they look at that food and say, "This is good, pleasant, and desirable." If you withhold this from them they will feel deprived.

They have come to believe the lie and are trapped into an endless cycle of defeat. They diet, but to no avail. They fundamentally believe that all that unhealthy food is good, pleasant, and desirable.

I have heard from pulpits for years that sin is *fun*, it is pleasant, and it is enjoyable. We must just deny ourselves.

We have got this thing all wrong. If you have the mind of Christ, then sin will never seem fun to you. It will never seem pleasant. It will never seem enjoyable.

The Bible declares:

> Therefore if any man be in Christ, he is a new creature: old things are passed away; behold, all things are become new.
>
> —2 CORINTHIANS 5:17, KJV

> Let this mind be in you, which was also in Christ Jesus.
>
> —PHILIPPIANS 2:5, KJV

> Forasmuch then as Christ hath suffered for us in the flesh, **arm yourselves likewise with the same mind**: for he that hath suffered in the flesh hath ceased from sin.
>
> —1 PETER 4:1, KJV

Do you see Jesus looking at sin with longing? No, I tell you, He hated sin. He had His mind so in line with the mind of the Father that even His senses were repulsed by sin. We too can live this way. We can so take on the mind of Christ that even our senses, our emotions, are repulsed by sin:

> But strong meat belongeth to them that are of full age, even those who by reason of use **have their senses exercised to discern both good and evil**.
>
> —HEBREWS 5:14, KJV

I personally have experienced this in my own life. When I got saved God delivered me from five years of heavy drug and alcohol use. He not only broke the power of the physical addiction off my life, but He forever removed the desire. I have never even wanted to touch a drug since that day.

What happened that so totally freed me that I would never return to that which used to dominate my life?

I had an experience!

I had an experience with the living Word that was so overwhelming, so strong, so good, pleasant, and desirable, that it forever changed the way I think.

Once I experienced the living reality of Christ deep enough, I now longed for Him more than for the drugs. I saw Christ as the thing to be desired, and to be without Him would be horribly painful. My emotions were now forever changed. What I used to long for, now I had a disdain for. In one night I was forever changed. In one night my emotions turned from driving me into sin and bondage, to driving me into the loving arms of Christ.

I now thought different. Therefore I felt different. Therefore I acted different.

Satan had lost his hold on me.

If you are going to walk in total victory, you must be able to locate your enemy and locate the battlefield.

Your greatest enemy is wrong thinking and the battlefield is your mind.

You may say, "I thought Satan was my greatest enemy." He is your enemy, but he has been defeated. If he can't get you to believe a lie, then he has *no* power over you at all. He is powerless to touch you if you have right, godly thinking.

The strategy of Satan, which hasn't changed throughout history, is the same: to get you to believe a lie to make you feel insecure and inferior. Then as your emotions of insecurity and inferiority begin to pulsate through your being, he will present to you another lie. He will show you something bad and convince you it is good, pleasant, and desirable to remove your insecurity and your inferiority.

Once you take of his fruit you then have again entered the trap and reinforced his control over your life.

CHAPTER 10

TRUE AND FALSE REPENTANCE

(For the weapons of our warfare are not carnal, but mighty through God to the pulling down of strong holds;) Casting down imaginations, and every high thing that exalteth itself against the knowledge of God, and **bringing into captivity every thought to the obedience of Christ**.

—2 CORINTHIANS 10:4–5, KJV

T AKING EVERY THOUGHT CAPTIVE is the key to total victory. The Scripture commands us to repent. Repenting is not necessarily boohooing and crying, snotting and spitting everywhere. I have seen a lot of people go through the emotional expressions of so-called repentance but never change. Once again they have fallen into the trap of wrong emotions based upon wrong thinking.

Often when the Lord truly deals deeply with you, there is a great flood of emotions including sorrow and remorse for the sin in which you've been involved. But many people think that just because they had the flood tide of emotions of sorrow and remorse, then they have repented. We say they were "broken". Pastors get excited when they see this, members rejoice, and the person under conviction feels like they are now right with God.

All of this is a great deception because, as of yet, this person hasn't repented. Although this expression of sorrow and remorse can be, and often is, the first step towards repentance, it isn't repentance by itself.

> For godly sorrow worketh repentance to salvation not to be repented of: but the sorrow of the world worketh death.
> —2 CORINTHIANS 7:10, KJV

Sorrow leads us to repentance, but isn't repentance by itself.

Repentance isn't an emotional expression. It's a change in the way we think.

The word *repent* means "to change ones thinking; to think differently." In order for repentance to be genuine, there must be a fundamental change in the way one thinks. If someone doesn't change the way they think, they will ultimately never change their actions. Their emotional desire for pleasure and avoidance of pain will drive them. They will once again fall into the trap of Satan.

Often I have seen people come into church and be greatly moved upon by the Spirit of the Lord. God genuinely convicts them of their sin. They are overcome by deep emotions of regret and sorrow. Everybody comes and hugs them at the altar and says, "Praise God you're saved," or "You've rededicated."

They feel loved and accepted. They like this feeling, so they come back to church the next service. Even though they still may not have fundamentally changed the way they think about sin, they might be willing to avoid some overt sins, because they want to be accepted by this new church peer group. They start going through the motions of religion, believing all along that they are born again.

They are feeling a new sense of security and value because of the peer acceptance. They begin to eat of the fruit of religion. If the desire for the acceptance of man is deep enough, and if enough of their value and security can come from this new peer group of church friends, they will be willing to change even more of their outward behavior.

All along they are being driven by this need for security and value. If they get it from the church group, they stay in church to feed this need. If their unsaved friends provide it more for them than the church group, they'll quickly return to their old lifestyle.

They never truly repented. They only started to eat a different piece of fruit from the same tree. Deep on the inside they still love sin and are bound by the trap of the tree. Insecurity and inferiority rule their emotional lives, thus dictating their actions.

In my experience I have seen many people come and stay in church for a season. The church they attend preaches surrender to God and an ever-deepening commitment to holy living. This starts producing a conflict within them. Although they love the sense of security and value they get from church, they start feeling condemned. They are still being convicted, but aren't repentant. These people begin to feel like they can't live this Christian life.

This conflict causes them to begin to feel insecure and inferior again. Once again the enemy offers them some fruit. For different people he offers different pieces.

For some he offers them the fruit of self-condemnation. They begin to verbally and mentally beat themselves up, saying to themselves, "I'm no good" or "I'm too weak". They begin to think that they will never make it and are emotionally driven right back out of the church.

For some the enemy offers the fruit of a critical spirit. They feel insecure and inferior so they begin to attack the church, the leaders, and the doctrine. They love to call them legalistic and judging. They love to think that the problem is everybody else. They say these people don't love enough, the pastor is too harsh, or the people don't understand what they are going through.

These believers will often leave and go to a church that "accepts them as they are." This usually refers to a church that won't preach righteous living, but a grace that doesn't require holiness.

Some will stay in their original church and gather a small group around them who also agree with them that the leadership is too harsh and unloving. This new group will help bolster their feelings. Once again they are being driven by insecurity and inferiority. They simply pick up a different piece of fruit to provide for themselves the feelings of security and value.

For some the enemy offers them the fruit of rebellion. They just blatantly begin to reject the Word and teachings of the church. They run back to their old lifestyles, to friends who will accept them the way they are.

And for some he offers them the fruit of religion. To deal with this growing sense of insecurity and inferiority, they hunker down and begin to "deny" their flesh. They'll focus on changing even more outward actions, so they can get the praises of men as to how much they have "grown in the Lord". They'll attend every service, change their dress and speech, pay their tithes, and do all their religious duties. Not only this, but they become zealots for outward expressions of holiness.

They'll begin to preach to others from their new found convictions and begin to belittle others for not conforming. This new found zeal feeds them with a sense of superiority and deepens their bondage. Others become the whipping post for these "preachers of holiness."

Depending on the church and organization, they may now start to be promoted. People who also are getting their sense of security and value from their outward righteousness begin to recognize the "call of God" on their lives and empower them to climb the ranks of church hierarchy.

The trap of the tree goes on and on.

Those who leave the church are now convinced that there is no real power inside the church to change them.

The fact is they never really repented.

The trap of the tree goes on and on.

True Repentance

Repentance is to change the way one thinks. If you think differently in accordance with the Word of God, then your feelings and emotions will line up with the Word of God and drive you in the right direction.

That is why the Scripture makes some very powerful statements about the person who has truly repented and been born again:

> Whosoever is born of **God doth not commit sin**;
> for his seed remaineth in him: and **he cannot sin**,
> because he is born of God.
>
> —1 JOHN 3:9, KJV

The Amplified Bible says "No one born (begotten) of God [deliberately, knowingly, and habitually] practices sin" (1 John 3:9, AMP).

One day while I was driving to a meeting in Sacramento, California, the Spirit of God began to speak to me about sin. He spoke to me a definition of sin that forever changed my life and has changed the lives of multitudes around the world.

He said, **"The essence of sin is the rejection of God's rightful authority over one's life."**

Everything in the kingdom of heaven is about authority.

The word *authority* speaks to us of the "legal right to exercise power."

When one has authority they have the legal right to exercise power over another.

My brother is a California Highway Patrol officer. One of the areas he patrols is the I-5 corridor through parts of central California. When he sees a motorist speeding he will quickly catch up to them and turn on that infamous red light. Most of the time the speeding motorist slows down and stops on the side of the road.

He'll get out of his car, and, as most of us have experienced, he'll ask for the driver's license and registration. The motorist, without question, will hand them over to him.

Why? Are they intimidated by him? He is six feet tall, but not that physically intimidating.

It is because they recognize that he has a legal right to pull them over and ask for their documentation. They have submitted to his legal right of authority. There came a moment that they made a decision. When the motorist saw the light they had to choose: Do I submit, or do I reject?

Do I accept this officer's legal right of authority, or do I reject it?

If the motorist decides to reject it, he can then choose to do any number of different actions. He could simply keep driving and ignore the light. He could try to speed away or even ram my brother's police car. He could pull over, jump out of his car and start cursing at my brother, or even try to attack him. But before he could choose to do any of these actions, he first had to decide that he wasn't going to accept my brother's legal right of authority to pull him over.

Sin is an authority issue. God created us and has an inherent right to tell us what to do, say, and how to live. He is LORD.

From the beginning all sin is based in this single first step: **the rejection of God's rightful authority**.

Lucifer in heaven had to first reject God's rightful authority before he could even consider defying Him.

The same is true with us. In order to disobey God, we must first reject His legal right of authority over us. We must say, "*No*, I will not submit to You. I reject Your legal rightful claims over my life and actions." Oh, we might not say it that boldly, but we all do it. You can't do any *action* of disobedience until you first reject God's legal, rightful authority over your life.

The Essence of Sin: The Rejection of God's Rightful Authority Over One's Life

Now the Bible commands us to repent of our sins. In other words, change the way we think about rejecting God's rightful authority and accept His rightful authority over our lives. This is true repentance.

That is why 1 John 3:9 (AMP) says, "He who is born of God does not deliberately, habitually, and knowingly continue to practice sinning (reject God's rightful authority)." The person who has truly repented has changed the rejection of God's rightful authority and has now chosen to submit to His authority. Once one chooses to submit, then all the power needed to live accordingly is released.

When we repent He will forgive us and *cleanse* us from all unrighteousness. (See 1 John 1:9.) He will cleanse us from all our un-God-like character and create in us His character and nature. The power of sin over our lives will be broken. As we take each area of our lives to God and surrender them to the rightful authority of Christ, then the power of redemption and deliverance begins to work practically in our daily actions.

It really makes since if you think about it. If I have truly repented, I have changed my thinking about rejecting God's rightful authority over a particular issue. I now not only submit, but I also agree with God that this thing is utterly sinful and worthy to be abhorred. My belief about the desirability of that particular sin now has changed. I not only agree that it is wrong, but I also believe and agree that it is not desirable. At this point my feelings about this sin now change from desire to disgust—from longing for it to wanting to leave it. As long as I agree with God's perspective of this sin, I will feel God's way about it. My emotions will then be God-like emotions and will drive me away from that sinful issue.

If you are still being drawn towards certain sins, it is because you have *not* truly and completely repented. You may feel very guilty and ashamed of your desires, but deep down you still love it. Deep down that sin is feeding some insecurity and/or inferiority, and the desire to feed that is greater than your willingness to submit to God's rightful authority.

CHAPTER 11

SPIRIT OF WISDOM AND REVELATION

But we all, with unveiled face, beholding as in a mirror the glory of the Lord, are being transformed into the same image from glory to glory, just as by the Spirit of the Lord.

—2 CORINTHIANS 3:18

ONE OF THE MOST transforming events of my life took place in February of 1987. I was saved only a few months, when inside of me arose a deep desire to pray for the ability to work the works of God supernaturally. As December of 1986 approached, a spirit of prayer came upon me for weeks.

I had been radically saved May 2, 1986, and instantly delivered from five years of drug addiction. Not only did God deliver me from the addiction, but forever removed the desire from me. Two days later while on my knees worshipping, God spoke to me and said, "I have called you to preach My gospel." He showed me, in a vision, all of my plans and dreams for my life. When I responded, "Yes Lord, I will." I saw my plans fade off in the distance, and then God gloriously baptized me in the Holy Spirit.

It didn't take long for me to realize that the church was lacking the one element that delivered me and was needed to deliver my generation: the supernatural power of God.

Although the ministry I got saved under moved in the power, so many didn't and I saw the negative results of that. I saw a lethargy and weakness. I saw people going to church, but having no victory in life.

As December of 1986 came upon me, a deep cry rose up, "God, I must have the power to reach my generation!" I began to pray more than four hours a day. I was focused on one thing. "God, give to me the power."

As the New Year rolled around, a friend of mine told me about a mighty man of God by the name of Morris Cerullo. He told me that he had never seen anybody move in such power. He talked about a world conference that Morris Cerullo held at the beginning of each year. My friend told me about how the glory of God would fill the whole hotel, and how people would be caught away into the Spirit in their rooms.

I was so intrigued that I asked to borrow a tape series by Dr. Cerullo called *Proof Producers*. My friend was hesitant to lend them, because he was afraid he would never get them back. Those of you who have "lent" books and tapes will relate to his concern. After much begging he loaned them to me.

I drove back home to San Diego, and on Thursday morning of the first week of January 1987, I sat down in front of my tape deck with my Bible opened ready to hear a good preaching message.

As Dr. Cerullo began to preach, I thought his voice was really raspy and the organ irritating. Then he said for us to look at our hands. He said, "The future success of the work of God lies in the hands of those who can answer this question. 'What must we do that we might work the works of God?'"

I was hooked. My Bible dropped to the floor as a wave of the Holy Spirit hit the crowd on the tape. That same wave hit me in my home. I began to cry out to God, "I must have the power!"

For the next three hours I listened to Dr. Cerullo preach as wave after wave of the Holy Spirit would hit, then Dr. Cerullo would continue to preach. With tears in my eyes I cried out, "This is it! This is it!" I knew in my heart of hearts this man had the anointing I needed.

I finished the first three hours of the tapes, and then went into my room to pray for an hour. I came out after prayer to listen to more of the tapes. I placed the next tape in when God spoke to me, "Pack your bags and go to the World Conference." I didn't know where it was, so I looked on the tape and saw an address, called information, and called the ministry five minutes before their offices closed.

They told me the conference had started Tuesday and was at the Hilton Hotel next to Disneyland.

I grabbed a grocery bag, threw in some clothes, wrote a note to my roommate, and left for the conference with only $50 to my name.

I arrived at the conference. Dr. Cerullo was already preaching. I sat in an overflow room and watched him on a giant screen. Just like on the tapes, waves of the Holy Spirit would sweep the room. I was overwhelmed by the manifested presence of God as Dr. Cerullo preached on the "Glory of God", the *doxa*.

A final wave of the Spirit hit the meeting. I was standing and crying out to God when I felt a giant hand from heaven come and lay hands on my head. Immediately I fell to the ground overpowered by the presence of God. I lay there quite a while. When I got up I told some people about my day. They immediately opened their hotel room to me. I was ready to sleep in my car and fast, because this was my breakthrough.

I could hardly sleep. I was up at 6:30 the next morning to go down for prayer. I sat in the main hall from 6:30 a.m. till 5:30 p.m. I didn't want to miss a thing.

Somehow I ended up on the front row for the evening service, and Jesus preached to us for three hours. Yes, it might have been the body of Morris Cerullo, but it was Jesus who preached to us about *agape*.

I sat there with my jaw to the floor knowing that this man had the anointing that could change a world.

God spoke to me to become a partner and learn at the feet of His servant.

I joined and a few weeks later they sent me the complete teaching by Dr. Cerullo from the conference on *Unity in the Spirit*. While listening to the tapes I saw a vision and received an anointing that forever changed my life and continues to change it today.

There was a section on the tapes where Dr. Cerullo preached from Ephesians 1:17–19. He spent seven to ten minutes preaching on it. As he preached something inside of me was so deeply stirred that I had to listen to that section over and over again. Each time I listened to it the presence of God would come on me. I knew there was something deeper here than I was at first seeing. So I listened over and over and prayed.

After about two hours of this my roommate came home. I tried to tell him what I was experiencing, but every time I started I would become overwhelmed and start crying.

Three times I tried. The third time it happened. As I tried to explain it, I had a full-blown open vision. I dropped to the ground and cried out, "I see it! I see it!"

What did I see?

> That the God of our Lord Jesus Christ, the Father of glory, may give to you the spirit of wisdom and revelation in the knowledge of Him.
>
> —EPHESIANS 1:17

The Amplified says it this way:

> [For I always pray to] the God of our Lord Jesus Christ, the Father of glory, that He may grant you a spirit of wisdom and revelation [of insight into mysteries and secrets] in the [deep and intimate] knowledge of Him.
>
> —EPHESIANS 1:17, AMP

This was not just the prayer of the Apostle Paul; it was the prayer of the Holy Spirit:

> **All Scripture is given by inspiration of God.**
>
> —2 TIMOTHY 3:16

The Holy Spirit told Paul what to pray:

> Knowing this first, that no prophecy of Scripture is of any private interpretation, for prophecy never

came by the will of man, but holy men of God spoke
as they were moved by the Holy Spirit.

—2 Peter 1:20–21

This prayer was from God for the most spiritual people
of Paul's day. This was not for the baby Christians. The
Ephesian church was the most mature group, and the
book of Ephesians is the deepest book on the purpose for
the existence of the church.

To these people Paul writes:

**[For I always pray to] the God of our Lord Jesus
Christ, the Father of glory, that He may grant you
a spirit of wisdom and revelation [of insight into
mysteries and secrets] in the [deep and intimate]
knowledge of Him.**

—Ephesians 1:17, AMP

Paul prays the prayer of the Holy Spirit that God the
Father would give to them a spirit of wisdom and revelation. Now there is only one Holy Spirit, so what he is
talking about here is an anointing—a supernatural power
for wisdom and revelation of **insight into mysteries and
secrets in the [deep and intimate] knowledge of Him.**

God has secrets and He wants to reveal them to us:

He who dwells in the **secret place of the Most High**
Shall abide under the shadow of the Almighty.

—Psalm 91:1

But **there is a God in heaven who reveals secrets**, and He has made known to King Nebuchadnezzar what will be in the latter days. Your dream, and the visions of your head upon your bed, were these:

—DANIEL 2:28

Then I will give them heart to know Me, that I am the LORD; and they shall be My people, and I will be their God, for they shall return to Me with their whole heart.

—JEREMIAH 24:7

But as it is written: **"Eye has not seen, nor ear heard, Nor have entered into the heart of man The things which God has prepared for those who love Him." But God has revealed them to us through His Spirit.** For the Spirit searches all things, yes, the deep things of God.

—1 CORINTHIANS 2:9–10

We need supernatural eyesight to see and understand the mysteries and secrets of God. God wants us to know His secrets:

And you will seek Me and find Me, when you search for Me with all your heart.

—JEREMIAH 29:13

Why does God want you to know His secrets?

> The secret things belong to the LORD our God, but
> **those things which are revealed belong to us** and
> to our children forever.
>
> —DEUTERONOMY 29:29

The secrets of the Lord belong to Him until they are revealed. Before I got saved, salvation was a mystery to me. I didn't know that I needed to be born again. But on May 2, 1986, the mystery of salvation was revealed to me, and if I simply yielded to it, I would be saved.

Many godly Christians die of sickness every day. They understand salvation, but the mystery of Isaiah 53:5 they haven't yet seen:

> But He was wounded for our transgressions, He was
> bruised for our iniquities; The chastisement for our
> peace was upon Him, **And by His stripes we are
> healed**.

Once the mystery of the healing power of Christ's stripes is revealed, then we have access to His healing power. When you *see* it, you can *have* it. Once the mystery is revealed it rightfully belongs to you. It is your inheritance. An inheritance that is not understood does the heir no good. It is not until the heir sees and understands what is rightfully his that he can have it.

In Ephesians Paul, by the Holy Spirit, is praying that God will give to you supernatural eyesight into mysteries and secrets in the deep and intimate knowledge of God. Because once you see the secrets, you have legal access to them. For we are "joint-heirs with Christ Jesus" (Rom. 8:17).

One of the jobs of the Holy Spirit is to show us the secrets of God:

> However, when He, the Spirit of truth, has come, **He will guide you into all truth**; for He will not speak on His own authority, but whatever He hears He will speak; and He will tell you things to come. He will glorify Me, for **He will take of what is Mine and declare it to you**.
>
> —JOHN 16:13

God wants to open your spiritual eyes to see—the eyes of your heart, your understanding:

> By having the eyes of your heart flooded with light, so that you can know and understand the hope of your calling.
>
> —EPHESIANS 1:18, AMP

Man has two sets of eyes. We have our natural eyes, but we also have our spiritual eyes. We will see things with our spiritual eyes that our natural eyes will never see. The prayer of the Holy Spirit is that "the eyes of your heart be flooded with light."

The Light of Jesus

> For it is the God who commanded light to shine out of darkness, who has shone in our hearts to give the **light of the knowledge of the glory of God** in the face of Jesus Christ.
>
> —2 Corinthians 4:6

It was at this point that the vision took hold of me. The light of the knowledge of the glory of God is revealed in the face of Jesus.

I saw in an open vision the Word of God. I saw these verses suspended in the air and from within the words themselves I saw a visible bright, blue-white light. It was the most beautiful light I had ever seen. It was the visible glory of God. I fell to my knees and cried out, "I see it! I see it!" Then God spoke to me and said, "Through My Word you'll see Me."

The spirit of wisdom and revelation came upon me and opened my eyes to see the mystery of the gospel, "which is **Christ in you the hope of glory**' (Col. 1:27, KJV).

This event changed my life and forever set the course of my ministry. It was the revelation of Christ that would change everything. As we see Him as He is, we will be changed. (See John 3:2.)

Eyes to See

By having the eyes of your heart flooded with light, so that you can know and understand the hope of your calling.

—Ephesians 1:18, AMP

Man has two sets of eyes. He has his natural eyes with which he perceives visually the world around him. Man also has spiritual eyes. These are the eyes of his heart, his understanding. With his spiritual eyes man will see things that are beyond the natural realm.

Man lives in two worlds. He lives in a natural world, but he also lives in a spirit world.

God wants to flood the eyes of our heart with light, "the light of the knowledge of the glory of God in the face of Jesus Christ" (2 Cor. 4:6).

It is at this point that a dimension of spiritual warfare takes place that breaks the hold of insecurity and inferiority off of our lives. The reason Eve was deceived into taking the fruit is because she lost *sight*—sight of the revelation of God, and thereby lost sight of who she was.

It is in this ability to see that all of our strength comes to defeat the enemy and close the door to insecurity and inferiority.

The only reason that we are subject to insecurity and inferiority is because we fail to see as God sees. This prayer of the Apostle Paul goes to the root of all our battles:

> [For I always pray to] the God of our Lord Jesus Christ, the Father of glory, that he may grant you a spirit of wisdom and revelation [of insight into mysteries and secrets] in the [deep and intimate] knowledge of Him. By having the eyes of your heart flooded with light, **so that you can know and understand the hope to which He has called you**.
>
> —EPHESIANS 1:17–18, AMP

Vision so that you can know and understand what is: the *hope* of your calling, the *hope* of your salvation, the *hope* of God's purpose for your life.

> To them God willed to make known what are the riches of the glory of this mystery among the Gentiles: **which is Christ in you, the hope of glory**.
>
> —COLOSSIANS 1:27

This is the root cause and solution to the problem. When we fail to see ourselves and others as God sees us, we become vulnerable to the spirits of insecurity and inferiority.

The prayer of the Holy Spirit through Paul goes to the solution needed. We must have supernatural eyes to see Him for three distinctive purposes. This will give us the power to fulfill our God-given purposes individually and corporately.

The first of these three areas is for you to **know and understand the hope of your calling**. This expresses itself in a couple of different ways.

If you ask most Christians what is their purpose here on the earth, they can't give you a very specific purpose. They may recite some scripture about witnessing or about showing forth the praises of God, but it is clear by their daily lives these are only words and not revelation.

You cannot truly understand your calling until you understand Jesus' calling.

Most Christians will tell you that the main purpose that Jesus came to the earth was to pay the price for our sins. I want to submit to you that He came for a much greater purpose, and that the work accomplished on the cross is much bigger than just forgiveness of sins.

Jesus in the Gospels and the Holy Spirit through the epistles make constant references to Christ's purpose:

> **I have come that they may have life**, and that they may have it more abundantly.
>
> —John 10:10

Just as the Son of Man did not come to be served, but to serve, and to give His life a ransom for many.
—MATTHEW 20:28

And this is eternal life, that they may know You, the only true God, and Jesus Christ whom You have sent. I have glorified You on the earth. **I have finished the work which You have given Me to do**.
—JOHN 17:3–4

That they all may be one, as You, Father, are in Me, and I in You; that they also may be one in Us, that the world may believe that You sent Me. **And the glory which You gave Me I have given them, that they may be one just as We are one**: I in them, and You in Me; **that they may be made perfect in one**, and that the world may know that You have sent Me, and have loved them as You have loved Me.
—JOHN 17:21–23

And the grand-slam purpose is found in 1 John:

For this purpose the Son of God was manifested, **that he might destroy the works of the devil**.
—1 JOHN 3:8, KJV

Jesus didn't just come to forgive us of our sins, but to fully restore to us *all* that was lost in the garden—to reconcile us back to our original purpose which can only be found in the revelation of God.

For God created man after His own image and in His own likeness. (See Genesis 1:27.) When man sinned he not only was kicked out of the Garden of Eden, but he also lost the connection to the glory of God. For man's purpose was not to just be a created being or to walk with God. God created man so He could eternally dwell in and express Himself through man.

God wanted to share all that He has and all that He is with another. So He created man. When man sinned, it separated him from God and thwarted the plans of God. So God immediately put a plan into place to not just forgive man, but to restore man back to His original purpose—to have another with whom to share Himself.

This is why Christ came; to restore man back to the place that the Father had always meant for him to have.

He wanted to share His glory with us. This is why Christ came, to restore the glory:

> **The mystery which has been hidden from ages and from generations, but now has been revealed to His saints**. To them God willed to make known what are the riches of the glory of this mystery among the Gentiles: **which is Christ in you, the hope of glory**.
>
> —Colossians 1:26–27

For in Him the whole fullness of Deity (the Godhead) continues to dwell in bodily form [giving complete expression of the divine nature]. **And you are in**

> **Him, made full and having come to fullness of life**
> **[In Christ you too are filled with the Godhead—**
> **Father, Son, and Holy Spirit—and reached full**
> **spiritual stature].**
>
> —COLOSSIANS 2:9–10, AMP

We must come into a revelation of the purpose of Christ to restore us back to the original purpose of God for our existence. We have been given the highest position of all in the universe. We have been predestined by God to be conformed into His image—to be like God:

> For whom He foreknew, He also predestined to be conformed to the image of His Son.
>
> —ROMANS 8:29

God designed us to be joined with Him as one for eternity:

> "For this reason a man shall leave his father and mother and be joined to his wife, **and the two shall become one flesh.**" This is a great mystery, **but I speak concerning Christ and the church**.
>
> —EPHESIANS 5:31–32

God has placed an irrevocable value upon us. He has set us at the highest position possible. He has placed on us the highest value possible. This revelation, when truly gotten by the body of Christ, will shatter all inferiority.

Remember, inferiority is the feeling of being lower in position or stature. The revelation of the hope of your calling, to be one with Christ, destroys the lie of inferiority.

Another area that "the hope of your calling" affects you is in your daily life. When you begin to understand the purpose of Christ, then the daily purpose of your life will also begin to come into focus. As long as we don't understand what we are called to here on the earth, we will live unfruitful, ineffective lives for the kingdom.

The lack of clear purpose opens the door for the enemy:

> Where there is no **vision**, the people **perish**: but he that keepeth the law, happy is he.
> —PROVERBS 29:18, KJV

The New King James version states it this way:

> Where there is no **revelation**, the people **cast off restraint**; But happy is he who keeps the law.
> —PROVERBS 29:18

When people lack clear vision, revelation, and purpose, they cast off restraint. Clear vision empowers man to be morally disciplined. The Apostle John states it this way:

> But we know that when He is revealed, we shall be like Him, for we shall see Him as He is. And everyone who has this hope in Him purifies himself, just as He is pure.
> —1 JOHN 3:2–3

In the world today many motivational speakers will teach you that you must have a clearly stated purpose in order to accomplish anything great. They have tapped into a characteristic that God placed in man. It is the driving force that clear purpose provides, that empowers men to do beyond what others think possible.

This quality of human nature, surrendered to the revelation of Christ, will empower us to excel in everything we set our hands to. Through the power of Christ and His Word in us there shall be nothing impossible:

> **If you abide in Me, and My words abide in you, you will ask what you desire, and it shall be done for you.**
>
>   —JOHN 15:7

Not only does God through the spirit of wisdom and revelation want us to know and understand the hope of our calling, but also **how rich is His glorious inheritance** in the saints. (See Ephesians 1:18.)

In order to reverse the work of Satan in the garden and forever close the door to the enemy, God also wants us to know that all that He has, has been given to us. There is nothing that God has that He has not given to the church. He placed a value on us that could never be matched and gave us everything that He has.

Joint Heirs

Jesus is the legal heir of all things:

> Has in these last days spoken to us by **His Son, whom He has appointed heir of all things**, through whom also He made the worlds; who being the brightness of His glory and the express image of His person, and upholding all things by the word of His power, when He had by Himself purged our sins, sat down at the right hand of the Majesty on high, **having become so much better than the angels, as He has by inheritance obtained a more excellent name than they**.
>
> —HEBREWS 1:2–4

And we are now joint heirs with Him:

> The Spirit Himself bears witness with our spirit that we are children of God, and if children, then heirs—heirs of God and joint heirs with Christ, if indeed we suffer with Him, that we may also be glorified together.
>
> —ROMANS 8:16–18

God has not withheld anything from us:

> He who did not spare His own Son, but delivered Him up for us all, how shall He not with Him also **freely give us all things?**
>
> —ROMANS 8:32

Whatever we ask in Jesus' name God has said He will give it to us:

> If you abide in Me, and My words abide in you, **you will ask what you desire, and it shall be done for you. By this My Father is glorified,** that you bear much fruit; so you will be My disciples.
>
> —JOHN 15:7–8

> And in that day you will ask Me nothing. Most assuredly, I say to you, **whatever you ask the Father in My name He will give you.** Until now you have asked nothing in My name. **Ask, and you will receive, that your joy may be full.**
>
> —JOHN 16:23–24

Many Christians have quoted these verses over and over again for years, but the reality is that they still haven't truly seen them work. So they go on about their business quoting and praying and not really seeing. Step by step the enemy causes us to question, "Does the Word really work?" Once gain he challenges the truthfulness of God.

Although many Christians wouldn't admit it, they don't really believe that whatever they ask for, in Jesus' name, God will do.

They waver in their hearts. The Bible states that those who doubt don't receive anything:

> But let him ask in faith, with no doubting, for he who doubts is like a wave of the sea driven and tossed by

the wind. **For let not that man suppose that he will receive anything from the Lord;** he is a double-minded man, unstable in all his ways.

—JAMES 1:6–8

It's one of Satan's great tricks. We pray while wavering and doubting. As a result we receive nothing, which reinforces our doubt, which leads to further unanswered prayers and a vicious cycle of defeat.

The problem goes back to a lack of revelation. A failure to see with spiritual eyes that everything God has, He has already given to us. It is our legal inheritance. We are joint heirs with Him.

Let's look at faith for a moment. The word *faith* comes from the Greek word *pistis* which means "fidelity or loyalty to an authority." Faith is not a feeling. It is a state of being. It is a loyalty to God and His Word. In the simplest terms it is a choice of the will to believe and obey God's Word, regardless of your circumstances.

We can only truly do this as we have a deepening revelation of Jesus. When we see Him, we become like Him. We are changed into His image and nature. We take on His characteristics.

Then, and only then, can we truly pray in faith and see that whatever we ask shall be done for us, in Jesus' name.

When we begin to see and understand that God has given to us all things and that we truly are joint heirs with Christ, then we will begin down the path of true freedom.

These truths must become more than words. They must become alive on the inside of us.

Unlimited Power

The third breakthrough that the spirit of wisdom and revelation gives to us is over all insecurity. It will give to us such confidence in Christ and His power that *nothing* will ever be able to shake us:

> And [so that you can know and understand] what is **the immeasurable and unlimited and surpassing greatness of His power in and for us** who believe, as demonstrated in the working of His mighty strength, which He exerted in Christ when **He raised Him from the dead and seated Him at His [own] right hand in heavenly [places].**
> —EPHESIANS 1:19–20, AMP, EMPHASIS ADDED

The same power that raised Christ from the dead, the unlimited supernatural power of God, is *in us* and is *for us*. The same power that said, "Let there be light," and there was light; the same power that upholds the universe; the same power that parted the Red Sea; the same power that sent fire down from heaven to consume Elijah's offering, delivered Daniel from the lions den, and destroyed the armies facing Gideon—that same power is *in* us. (See Gen. 1:3, Col. 1:17, Exod. 14:21, 2 Kings 1:10, Dan. 6:22, Judges 7:15.).

> Now to Him who is able to do exceedingly abun-
> dantly above all that we ask or think, **according to
> the power that works in us...**
>
> —EPHESIANS 3:20

> But we have this treasure in earthen vessels, that
> the excellence of the power may be of God and not
> of us.
>
> —2 CORINTHIANS 4:7

How often does the enemy, through our circumstances, make us feel powerless? We feel like there is nothing that we can do. We feel out of control.

This is the very purpose of terrorism—to make people feel so powerless over the violence that they simply surrender. The feeling of powerlessness is so unsettling that people will do just about anything to get a sense of power and security back, even if that means surrender.

Why, during World War II, did whole countries surrender to Germany? They were afraid that they didn't have the power to defeat them. They were afraid that if they tried, they would suffer greater loss than to simply surrender.

So many countries, after being attacked, simply surrendered control to the Germans. This is what happened to many Jews. At first they moved the Jews into the slums. The Jews, as a whole, went along with this. Even though it was a level of bondage, they figured it was better than dying.

They saw the strength of the German army and felt that they could not defeat them in battle. Therefore they had only two choices: die or surrender.

So the majority surrendered. Step by step the German control deepened, and the freedoms of the Jews were stripped away layer by layer.

Each step they faced the two choices: fight and possibly die or surrender. Most continued down the path of surrender.

We have seen this repeated time and again throughout history with many nations and peoples.

The oppression continued. The Germans took the Jews from the slums and started to place them in "labor camps," better know as concentration camps.

The bondage deepened, the suffering increased, and the death they tried to avoid through surrender crept up upon them.

The same is happening in the spirit realm today. The enemy has been attacking the Christians. He has been threatening them through insecurity and inferiority. He has convinced many, including preachers, that as long as we are here on this earth the *flesh* can never be conquered.

We hear time and again that as long as we are in the flesh, we will sin. We have already begun down the path of surrender. Step by step the enemy will deepen his control and increase our suffering.

We have believed the lie that the power of the cross is

not sufficient. We have believed that the power of sin is too great, and the best we can hope for is to avoid some sins.

We are so convinced that we can't win, that we easily give up. We just accept certain "struggles" in our lives as part of who we are. In an attempt to spiritualize it, we even say that this is "my thorn in the flesh." (See 2 Corinthians 12:7.)

Step by step the enemy gains deeper control through fear and intimidation, leading us to the spiritual gas chambers of a defeated life. We willingly follow his commands, because in our hearts we don't believe we have the power to defeat the enemy.

The devil is a liar!

Jesus said:

> Behold, I give you the authority to trample on serpents and scorpions, and **over all the power of the enemy, and nothing shall by any means hurt you.**
>
> —LUKE 10:19

> Assuredly, I say to you, **whatever you bind on earth will be bound in heaven, and whatever you loose on earth will be loosed in heaven.** "Again I say to you that if two of you agree on earth concerning anything that they ask, it will be done for them by My Father in heaven. For where two or three are gathered together in My name, I am there in the midst of them."
>
> —MATTHEW 18:18–19

We have been give power and authority—the right to exercise the miracle working power of God.

Not only does the enemy keep us in the bondage of sin because we lack a revelation of the power that is in and for us who believe, but he also keeps us from bringing to the world the resurrection power of Christ. We say things like, "I don't have the gift of healing or the power to work miracles. God has given that to a select few like Morris Cerullo or Benny Hinn."

The devil is a liar. Jesus said:

> And these signs will [**not maybe, but will**] follow those who believe: In My name they **will cast out demons;** they **will speak with new tongues;** they **will take up serpents;** and if they drink anything deadly, it will by no means hurt them; **they will lay hands on the sick, and they will recover.**
>
> —MARK 16:17–18, EMPHASIS ADDED

The spirit of wisdom and revelation will give you access to the power to defeat the enemy and to show the world that Jesus is who He claims to be.

Praise be to God! The fullness of Christ and His power has been given to us. He is in us. There is no power in hell or on earth that can overpower what is in us. We are totally secure because of Him who lives in us:

You are of God, little children, and have overcome them, because **He who is in you is greater than he who is in the world.**

—1 JOHN 4:4

No weapon formed against you shall prosper, And every tongue which rises against you in judgment You shall condemn. This is the heritage of the servants of the LORD, And their righteousness is from Me," Says the LORD.

—ISAIAH 54:17

God wants to give to you the spirit of wisdom and revelation so you will know the hope of your calling, your inheritance, and the power that is in and for you. As the revelation of Christ continues to work in you, it will eradicate every open door the enemy has to root insecurity and inferiority. Without those two roots all the other demon spirits have nothing to hold on to, and their power is easily broken.

CHAPTER 13

WALK FREE

THE REVELATION OF INSECURITY and inferiority will continue to grow in your life. As God opens your eyes you will see it work and how it affects so much of what we do.

The power of the revelation of Christ to break this stronghold cannot be underestimated. That is why the one thing the enemy fights the most in our lives and churches is to keep the true depth of the revelation of Christ from us.

Satan has done a masterful job of getting the church side tracked into programs and church growth concepts that appease the masses, but truly do little to bring people to the place of the depths of revelation of Christ Jesus that will free them.

This is not a surface experience. It will not come to you by simply going to church on Sunday mornings, attending an occasional Bible study, paying your tithes, and being a good person.

The place that we *all* need to go is much deeper in the Spirit, and this place is only found by those who truly seek the riches of His glory:

> But without faith it is impossible to please Him, for he who comes to God must believe that He is, **and that He is a rewarder of those who diligently seek Him.**
> —HEBREWS 11:6

> **Draw near to God and He will draw near to you.** Cleanse your hands, you sinners; and purify your hearts, you double-minded.
> —JAMES 4:8

There is a requirement of passion and pursuit of holiness that is needed to see the mysteries and secrets of God:

> Pursue peace with all people, and holiness, **without which no one will see the Lord.**
> —HEBREWS 12:14

> **Blessed are the pure in heart, For they shall see God.**
> —MATTHEW 5:8

Much of the modern day church is more interested in having an enjoyable service, a good children's program, and friends than they are in pursuing a deep, surrendered, committed relationship with God. We have become comfortable in our lethargy and committed to our complacency.

The problem in the world today is not that there is too much sin or evil. There is too little Jesus revealed.

Light dispels darkness, and the light of the revelation of Christ destroys the darkness of this world.

This is the battle of our lives, the battle of our minds. Whose words will dominate and control the way we think? Whoever controls the mind of a man controls that man.

If the thoughts of insecurity and inferiority rule even part of your thinking, then the enemy has a stronghold upon which he *will* launch further assaults. If the thoughts of Christ rule your mind, then you will be truly free in every area.

Take time to reread this book and meditate on the truths and scriptures presented. Let the Holy Spirit explode understanding inside of you, so you can truly begin down the path of freedom.

Satan has not changed his tactics since the beginning. It's the exact same plan of attack. Once identified and dealt with through the spirit of wisdom and revelation, the victories that we will walk in shall be astounding.

Christ will truly be formed in us and the world will see that:

> **If the Son makes you free, you shall be free indeed.**
>
> —John 8:36